John Davidson

Bruce

A drama in five acts

John Davidson

Bruce
A drama in five acts

ISBN/EAN: 9783337303969

Printed in Europe, USA, Canada, Australia, Japan

Cover: Foto ©Thomas Meinert / pixelio.de

More available books at **www.hansebooks.com**

BRUCE

BOOKS BY JOHN DAVIDSON.

THE NORTH WALL. 1884. Glasgow: Wilson & McCormick.
Transferred by the Author to the present publishers (2s. 6d. net).

BRUCE: A DRAMA. 1886. Glasgow: Wilson & McCormick.
Transferred by the Author to the present publishers (5s. net)

SMITH: A TRAGEDY. 1888. Glasgow: Fred. W. Wilson & Brother.

PLAYS. 1889. Greenock: John Davidson.
Transferred by the Author to the present publishers (5s. net).

N.B.—A few Copies of this Book were issued in 1890 with the imprint of Mr. T. Fisher Unwin, under the title of "Scaramouch in Naxos, a Pantomime, and other Plays."

PERFERVID. 1890. London: Ward & Downey.

MONTESQUIEU'S "LETTRES PERSANES," A TRANSLATION, with Introduction and Notes. 2 vols. 1891. London (published by J. C. Nimmo, but without his imprint).

THE GREAT MEN AND A PRACTICAL NOVELIST. 1891. London: Ward & Downey.

N.B.—"A Practical Novelist" is "The North Wall," with some slight revision and the last chapter omitted.

IN A MUSIC HALL, AND OTHER POEMS. 1891. London: Ward & Downey.

FLEET STREET ECLOGUES. 1893. London: Elkin Mathews and John Lane (5s. net). *Second Edition.*

BAPTIST LAKE. 1893. London: Ward & Downey. *In the Press.*

BRUCE

A Drama in Five Acts

BY

JOHN DAVIDSON

AUTHOR OF "THE NORTH WALL"

LONDON
ELKIN MATHEWS *and* JOHN LANE
THE BODLEY HEAD, VIGO STREET
1893

TO

My Friend,

DAVID PATON, ESQ.

DRAMATIS PERSONÆ.

ROBERT BRUCE, *Earl of Carrick, afterwards King of Scotland.*
EDWARD BRUCE.
NIGEL BRUCE.
LAMBERTON, *Archbishop of St. Andrews.*
WALTER, *the Steward of Scotland.*
SIR WILLIAM WALLACE.
SIR JAMES DOUGLAS.
SIR THOMAS RANDOLF.
SIR CHRISTOPHER SETON.
SIR JOHN SETON.
JAMES CROMBE.
KIRKPATRICK.
COMYN, *Earl of Badenoch.*
COMYN, *Earl of Buchan.*
MACDUFF, *Earl of Fife.*
SIR ROBERT COMYN.

EDWARD I., *King of England.*
EDWARD II., *King of England.*
The Earl *of* PEMBROKE.
Lord HENRY PERCY.
Lord ROBERT CLIFFORD.
SIR INGRAM DE UMFRAVILLE.
SIR GILES DE ARGENTINE.
SIR PETER MALLORIE, *Justiciary of England.*
HUGH BEAUMONT.
ISABELLA, *Countess of Carrick, afterwards Queen of Scotland.*
ISOBEL, *Countess of Buchan.*
Countess *of* BADENOCH.
Lady DOUGLAS.

An Old Man, a Young Friar, a Messenger, a Forester, a Spy. Lords, Ladies, Gentlemen, Monks, Soldiers, etc.

Scene :—LONDON and SCOTLAND.

BRUCE.

ACT I.

Scene I.—London. *A Room in the Palace.*
King Edward I., Earl of Pembroke,
Lord Henry Percy, *and* Lord Robert
Clifford.

Edward I.   Once more, my lords, the rude
    north claims our care.
A faction there is still opposed to peace,
Strongly ill-willed to England and to me,
Obdurate, set, incorrigibly wroth—
A band whose blood is of the liquid flame
That often madly jets in savage veins,
When wisdom would bestow some blessed
    gift,
Some pearl which ignorance rejects with scorn,

And chafes and frets and sets the world on
    fire.
The Bruce, my lords, has fled the English
    court:
He goes to Scotland, and his guiding star
Is that same beacon of rebellious light
Built up by every burning Scottish heart.
Astonishment and curious desire
Shouldering each other in your eyes I see,
Like townsmen gazing from a window's height
At some strange pageantry afoot below;
There let them crowd, for wonders are to pass.
Were I to ask you, now, if Bruce or Comyn
Has played the fairer game you might say this:
They cannot be compared—Bruce always
    with,
And Comyn always opposite to me;
Yet have they both held by the cause they
    chose,
So there's a parity of constancy.
Such answer might be yours. Then I would
    say,
They both are faithless: here I hold the proof.
                           [*Exhibits a scroll.*

This is a deed transferring Bruce's lands
To Comyn, who exchanges for the same
His claim—it's written so—to Scotland's
 crown.
He promises besides to aid the Bruce
To gain the state and name of King of Scots.
There are their signatures.

Pembroke. How chances it
That this indenture lies in your royal hands?

Edward I. John Comyn sent it me. You
 see—base rogues!—
Bruce false to me, and Comyn false to Bruce.

Pembroke. My liege, Bruce hitherto has
 borne a name
As bright and glorious as his golden shield,
Untarnished by dishonour's rusty breath.
This paper may be forged.

Edward I. That was my thought;
And so I had a copy of it made,
And sent to Bruce last night. My messenger

Asked, being charged so far, some word from
    him.
He half denied; but compromised, and craved
Three days to answer. So much grace I gave.
This is the first day, and last night he fled.

Pembroke. A sign of guilt. What will your
    highness do?

Edward I. With your good counsel, lords,
    doubtless, the best!

Percy. To horse, and take the knave alive
    or dead!

Edward I. A speedy finish; but consider
    this:
Comyn and Bruce divide the land of Scots;
They now are mortal foes; why need we stir
To fight two cocks who will each other slay
Between the high walls of their Scottish pit?
Yet Pembroke, Clifford, and bold Harry Percy
Be ready at a word to lead your knights
Across the border.

Percy.   Nor can that summons come
Too soon for Harry Percy.

Pembroke.   Nor for Pembroke.

Clifford.   And Clifford will not be the last to
   hear.

Edward I.   I would prefer that your alacrity,
Pleasing and comfortable as it is,
Were from the proof removed a farther cast:
And so were Wallace wise as he is wight
It would be.   Twice I offered grace and love,
If he would govern Scotland in my name.
He thanked me for my grace and for my love,
But at my terms he laughed as at a jest.
Had he accepted them, I say again,
As there is none so fit to rule the Scots,
Your willing service had been hardly asked.

Percy.   Let me say this : had such a league
   been struck
Between your highness and the valiant Scot,
You might have borne your banners through
   the world.

Pembroke. What specious arguments could
    Wallace urge?

Edward I. O, ask me not! My patience
    served me ill
To hear him out. How can I then rehearse
His saucy reasons, wasting breath and wrath!
Within short space you all shall hear himself;
A fortnight hence, I think, he will be tried.
And now, Lord Clifford, James of Douglas
    comes
To claim his father's lands, which you possess.
Tell me, who knows, what kind of man he is,
That we may judge how he will bear himself?

Clifford. A man of men, although my mortal
    foe.
I knew him well in Paris ere these broils.
Unarmed, a gentle blitheness graced his style:
A dainty lisp engaged his auditors
With tickling pleasure; such a piquant touch
Was in the Scottish Hector, as they called
    him,
Tripping with helpless tongue, like rose-lipped
    girls.

But when he armed his body, then his soul
Was harnessed in a dress of adamant :
His gentle look, hard-tempered to a frown,
With gloom could shade the thund'rous scowl
    of heaven ;
His voice was like a lion's ; and his arm
Wielded his sword with lightning speed and
    force.
In council-halls, o'er ladies' lutes, in war,
Brave, courteous, wise, loyal to truth, he was :
So is he: Douglas changes but for good.

Edward I. You praise him highly. You
    shall answer him.
He comes. Make room.

    (*Enter* SIR JAMES DOUGLAS.)

    We know your errand, sir.
Speak, and Lord Clifford here will answer
    you.

Douglas. Lord Clifford will, and must: be
    sure of that.
I also crave King Edward's open ear.

Clifford will reckon with me for my land:
You, sire, must render an account of blood.

Clifford. Clifford has yet to learn why
    Douglas dare
Speak such a swift defiance.

Edward I. (*turning his back to* DOUGLAS.)
    Answer him
On this wise, my good lord :—Your father, sir,
A faithless felon, died a prisoner
In Edward's dungeon ; and his forfeit lands
Reverted to the crown. It pleased the king
To make me lord of Douglasdale. Go, then,
Buy land where'er you may, I keep my own.
He has his answer, follow me, my lords.

  [*Exeunt* EDWARD I., PEMBROKE, CLIFFORD,
        and PERCY.

Douglas. There's justice in the heavens if
    not in kings !
He might have listened. It is very plain
King Edward means to play the tyrant now.

Yet tyrants can be courteous. Insolent!
To toss an answer o'er his shoulder at me,
Whetting with crude affront, the pointed
   "No,"
As one would check a cringing beggar's plea.
One way is left, a flinty, narrow way,
The rebel's way, the way I still have shunned:
And yet it seems not hard, but easy, broad,
Since I elect to be a traveller there.
Now though it be as hopeless as to stem
The Solway's tide, or toss the deep-based
   Bass
From Forth to France, with all my strength
   I'll fight
Against this tyrannous usurping king.
How strange that I should find rebellion's
   storm
The happy haven where my troubles end!
But so it is: my cares are blown away;
Light-hearted vigour is my lot once more;
And trampled conscience, like the heath
   released,
Springs up, and breathes sweet scent of ap-
   probation.
                               [*Exit.*

SCENE II. — DUMFRIES. *The Greyfriars Church.*

Enter BRUCE *and* COMYN OF BADENOCH.

Comyn. I thought you were in London, cousin mine.

Bruce. And still would have me there, or anywhere,
But by your side.

Comyn. Why is your tongue so harsh,
Your eye so big, your face so dimmed with ire?

Bruce. Why falter you? Why has your colour fled?
Why, but because my tongue still speaks its thought;
Because my face wears not the darker show
Of death's grimace upon a spear's long neck,
Grotesquely ornamenting London Bridge;

Because my limbs are not the bait of crows,
The gazing-stock of crowds in Scotland's
    towns;
Because I live and am at liberty:
These are the reasons why you tremble now.

Comyn. Not so; it is because I think you
    mad:
These monstrous breathings are insanity:
You shake with passion, hissing out your
    words.
I fear you; and I will have witnesses,
Or no more conference.
                         [*Going.*

Bruce. (*seizing his arm.*) With honest men
God is sufficient witness. Are you true?
You know my ground of wrath as well as I.

Comyn. Your words are like your brow,
    darker than night.

Bruce. Be this the sun that shall illumine
    them.
                      [*Exhibits a scroll.*

Sun, said I! rather inky light of hell,
Whereby you may behold your treachery.
I see it's true what I have heard of men,
Who, knowing right, pursue a wrongful course :
Custom uprears athwart the source of shame
A fragile dam; but when another marks
The waves that beat behind, they swell and burst
The sandy sea-wall of hypocrisy,
Like a packed gulf delivered by the moon.
That flood is in your face : you blush like fire.

Comyn. I blush to be accused of this great wrong.

Bruce. Comyn, you lie. Look, see, the very words
Of that compact, which we with aching hearts
Drew up and signed and swore in Stirling town.
Have you forgotten how we wept hot tears
Condoling over Scotland's misery?

Its fertile plains that richer were than gold,
Burnt up with fire, salted with tears and
   blood;
Its cots and palaces confounded low
In stony litters that the soil reclaims;
Its wealthy towns and pleasant places sacked;
Its people?—Ah! we could not sound our
   grief
For wives made widows; husbands, left
   alone;
And children, blighted by too early bareness
Of parents' comfortable snowy wisdom:
Death and destruction feasting everywhere.
We found ourselves to blame; therefore we
   wept,
Repenting of our jealousy and strife.
This pact united us in friendship's bond
For ever to oppose the English rule.
We prayed that our conjunction, like two
   stars
Meeting auspiciously for Scotland's weal,
Might yield its war-worn people prosperous
   peace;
And o'er the border cast calamities

Of such deserved and overwhelming woe,
That England never more should be inclined,
Nor have the power to wage a conquering
    war.
We then embraced, and you with trembling
    breath
Thanked God that Bruce and Comyn now
    were friends.
Two copies of our compact we endorsed.
Here is a third that's neither yours nor mine:
King Edward sent it me; whence had he it?

Comyn. Unless King Edward sent it back
    to you,
You having given it him, I cannot tell.

Bruce. God keep my hands from blood! O
    soulless wretch!
Obtuse, unthinking liar! Could I note
The shape of good that dances in your brain
To be matured for service by denial,
Perhaps that might extenuate your lie.
But knowing nothing save your treachery,
And hardened daring of a damning fact,

Relentless hate expels all dreams of love
That harboured once toward you within my
    heart.

Comyn.   If, then, your rage is for the present
    spent,
A few plain words may hope for audience.
What proof have you that Edward had this
    writ
Through me or mine? Impartial sense would
    blame,
Not me, who ever have been Scotland's friend,
And foremost in opposing Edward's power,
But you the truckling lord, inheriting
And practising your father's policy,
Which was to follow at the Longshanks' heel,
And fawn for smiles, and wait his highness'
    whim
To pay the lacqueying with a dirty crown.

Bruce.   This idle mockery becomes you well.
Did any doubt remain of your dark sin,
The hunting out a mote within my eye
To poise the beam that does disfigure yours,
Would make me sure.

Comyn. What legal proof, I say?

Bruce. The laws of God, honour, and loyalty
Condemn you traitor to their interests.
I judge you guilty, for I know right well
King Edward never had this scroll from me,
And no one else could give it him but you.
Your heart condemns you, though you brave
    it thus.

Comyn. And yet I say again, I swear by
    heaven,
I never saw that paper till to-day.

Bruce. Talk not of seeing!—Come to the
    altar here.
               [*They advance to the altar.*

Now lay your hand upon the traitorous sheet,
Call God to witness that you speak the truth,
And swear once more you have not broken
    faith.
Beneath your feet the dust of true men rests,
Your ancestors and mine; this lofty roof,

These consecrated walls and columns high
Are wont to hear the sounds of sacred song,
The gospel of the holy Christ of God;
This in God's house; this altar is God's throne.
Now, can you swear? You will not do it, sure.

Comyn. And what shall hinder me while I have breath?
Without my instigation or connivance
Our compact reached the King. If God's in heaven,
And I speak false, may I this moment die.

Bruce. (*stabbing* COMYN, *who falls.*) God is in heaven, and my hand wields his wrath! . . .
What have I done? A madman's dreadful deed!
I was engulfed, and now I'm cast ashore.
O, in our passionless, reflective hours
We lock emotion in a glass-walled jail
Of crisp philosophy; or give it scope
As far as Will, the turnkey, may allow

B

The chain of prudence to enlarge its steps!
But to some sense a small distraction comes—
Across the sight a butterfly, a flower—
The fetters snap, the prison crumbles—off!—
To clasp the air where shone our will-o-wisp!
For no gewgaw have I burst reason's bonds,
But to avenge a gross iniquity
That clamoured brazenly to heaven and earth.
O, it was human!—It was devilish!
Here, on the altar—O, the sacrilege!
That man of my own blood, whom I adjured
By every holy thing, to speak no wrong,
I do wrong, slaying. O, heinous sacrilege!—
Perhaps he is not dead. Comyn, look up;
Speak; make some sign. Alas! that fatal blow
Was aimed too surely at my cousin's heart!
I used God's name too when I struck him dead!
O horrid blasphemy! The sacrilege!
[*Going.*

[*Enter* KIRKPATRICK.

Kirkpatrick. My Lord!

Bruce.   I fear I have slain Comyn.   [*Exit.*

Kirkpatrick.   Ha!
You fear!—Then I'll make sure.   He opes his eyes.

Comyn.   False—foolish—dying—guilty—perjured—lost!
[*Dies.*

Kirkpatrick. (*stabbing Comyn.*) Something to staunch your muttering.   No fear, now.

[*Enter* SIR ROBERT COMYN *with his sword drawn.*

Robert Comyn.   Stop villain!   Hold your hand, rash murderer!

Kirkpatrick.   I only gave a grace-thrust to your nephew
To end his agony.   Put up your sword.
He died a good death on the altar-steps.

Robert Comyn.   Kirkpatrick, you have aided in a deed,
Unseconded, even in these fearful times.

Kirkpatrick.   Strong words and stiffly spoken. Does your sword
Keep pace with your sharp tongue?

Robert Comyn.   We'll try.

Kirkpatrick.   Come on!

[*They fight and* ROBERT COMYN *falls.*

Robert Comyn.   Is this the day of judgment for our house?
Kinsman, I was your follower on earth,
And now I am your henchman through death's vale.
[*Dies.*

[*Enter* EDWARD BRUCE, SIR CHRISTOPHER *and* SIR JOHN SETON, *and other gentlemen.*

Sir Christopher Seton.   Two Comyns dead!
Bruce only spoke of one.

Kirkpatrick. I slew the other. He would
  have me fight.

Sir John Seton. Alas! and could it be no
  other way?
There was enough dissension in the realm
Without a feud between these families,
Highest in state, and strongest in the field.

1st. Gentleman. Comyn is dead, and Bruce
  has laid him low.
The dead may slay the living. What say
  you?

2nd. Gentleman. I say so too. The stroke
  that Comyn killed
May yet recoil upon his murderer.

Edward Bruce. Judge not, my friends. A
  murder has been done
With outward signs of most unrighteous
  wrath.
But think who did the deed—the noblest
  Scot,

The knightliest chevalier, the kindliest friend,
The prince of brothers. I, who know, say
    this.
The very horror and the sacrilege
That frame the crime with dreader circum-
    stance,
Cry out the doer was insane the while,
And recommend him to your lenience.
Therefore, take warning; and before you
    judge
Let your bloods cool, lest you be guilty too
Of foolish rashness in your condemnation.
My brother left a message for you all :
He asks you who are friends to visit him
To-morrow at Lochmaben ; where he means
To lay the matter of his crime before you,
And take your counsel on the consequence.

1st Gentleman. It's fair we should withhold
    our judgment, sirs,
Until we be possessed of this event,
The cause and manner of its happening.

[*Shouting within. Enter* NIGEL BRUCE.

Nigel Bruce. The people want a leader, crying out,
"Down with the Southron! Let us take the castle!"
The news of Comyn's death has made them mad;
If blood were wine, and they had drunk of it
To fulness, they could not be more mature
For any mischief that the time suggests.

Edward Bruce. Good mischief, if the English suffer it.
I'll be their captain. Cæsar pricked his horse
Across the Rubicon defying Rome.
Bruce pricked John Comyn over death's dark stream
Defying England. Cæsar triumphed: Bruce
Shall triumph too, and now begins the fight.
Down with the Southron! Bruce for Scotland! Ho!
                                      [*Exeunt.*

SCENE III.—*The Same. Monks enter and lay the bodies side by side. A bell tolls,*

*and the monks kneel round the altar.
Then enter the* COUNTESS OF BADENOCH,
and COMYN, EARL OF BUCHAN, *and the*
COUNTESS OF BUCHAN.

Buchan. You holy men give place a little
while.

A Monk. To whom?

Buchan. The wife and friends of slaughtered
Comyn.

[*The monks retire.*

Countess of Badenoch. Would any mortal
think to look at me
This dead man was my husband? Should I
weep,
And rend with sighs my breast, and wring
my hands;
Peal out my sorrow, like a vesper bell
Calling the cloistered echoes' shadowy choir
To take the burden of a woeful dirge;
Enrobe myself in that dishevellment

Which tyrannous grief compels his subjects
    pale
To show their vassalage by putting on,
I might persuade myself and you, my friends,
That I am sorry for my husband's death :
Even as an actor, lacking any cue,
Visible, tangible, as I have here,
Steps lightly at a word upon the stage,
Leaving his brothers and their merry chat,
And takes upon him any passion's show
With such devotion and abandonment,
That what was first a cloak becomes a soul,
And audience and actor both are held
Dissolved in ecstasy ; which, breaking, back
From high heroics to sad homeliness
Their spirits are precipitated straight.
But I'll not play the broken-heart, for you,
My friends, my audience, know the cause I
    have
Rather to laugh than weep. O wretched
    corpse !
What habitation holds the spirit now,
Which Bruce ejected rashly, warrantless,
Pulling the house about the tenant's ears ?

Buchan.   He loved me little, and he loved
            you less ;
And by his death he leaves a legacy,
The taking up of which, if spirits watch
From where eternally they rest or pine,
Our tragic, many-scened mortality,
Will reconcile him to his sudden death.

Countess of Buchan.   Husband, what legacy ?

Buchan.   A mortal feud.

Countess of Buchan.   Will you avenge on
            Bruce the death of him
Whom his best friends lament not ?

Buchan.   Yes, I must.
And good Sir Robert, too—his blood cries
            out.
It is a duty that the world will look
To see performed directly and with speed,
Admitting no perfunct, half-passive dance
On patient providence.   Dissuade me not,
For it becomes you not.   There is a thing

That vaguely circulates in certain spheres
Concerning you, my dearest. Sad am I
That from my lips it first should taint your
    ears;
But you must know it now. Give me your
    hand.
This white and fragrant palm from guilty
    deeds,
That harden more than penitential toil,
Or from the touch of slime, is not more free,
Than your unshriven soul from infant
    thoughts
Swaddled in shame. But foul-tongued
    calumny,
Tutored by hatred, like a jabbering bird
With implication lewd repeats your name
And Bruce's in a breath.

Countess of Buchan.   Alas, I know!
The lying scandal that benights my life
Will be a foil to make my memory shine.—
If it confronts you graven on the sky
To visit retribution on his head
Whose hand laid low your cousin's, be it so:

I'll not invade your secrets ; but I mean
To do what woman can for Bruce's cause,
Which whispers tell me will be Scotland's
  soon.

Buchan.   Well, we'll not quarrel.   We'll talk
  of this again.

Countess of Badenoch.   Come, take me home.
  I'm in a gentler mood.
Let those good cowls return and pray their
  best.

[*Exeunt the* COUNTESS OF BADENOCH, *and
  the* COUNT *and* COUNTESS OF BUCHAN.
  *The monks advance and kneel, and the
  scene closes.*

ACT II.

Scene I.—Lochmaben. *A Room in the Castle. Enter* Lamberton, Archbishop of St. Andrews, Edward *and* Nigel Bruce, *the two* Setons, Sir Thomas Randolf, *and other lords and gentlemen.*

Lamberton. My lords and gentlemen, this is no time
For ceremony, which, when lazy peace
Has rusted o'er the world's slack businesses,
Oils easily the motion of affairs;
For now events impel each other on,
And higher powers than beadles usher them.
I am commissioned by the noble Bruce
To greet you heartily and wish you well,
While you remain within Lochmaben's walls.
By my advice he begs you to excuse
His absence, while I speak. When you have heard

I doubt not that you will. He has confessed
The sacrilegious crime of yesterday,
Contritely and with simple truthfulness.
No exculpation, no defence at all,
Such as we know there is, he offered me.
Some of us here may hold that Bruce's act
Should rather be extolled than stigmatized.
We know for certain now what was the wrong
That Comyn having wrought denied on oath,
And all our sympathy goes out to Bruce.
But such is the deceitfulness of sin
That feelings of the sweetest comfort oft
Mislead us to embrace iniquity.
Man's worst of deeds God turns to good
    account.
A penance, which I hope will work God's
    will,
I have enjoined on the humiliate earl;
A labour as transcendent in its kind
As ever travailed hero Hercules.
I mean to crown him, Robert, King of Scots:
His task will be to make that title good.
Now I have said a word that stirs your blood,
Begetting hope and courage, valiant twins.

And yet it is not I that speak, but God :
Surely God speaks. The sequence of events,
Of which this conference is the latest bud,
Appears to me a heavenly oracle,
As evident as Aaron's sprouting rod,
Commanding Robert Bruce to be the King.
He would have placed the crown on Comyn's head,
Had Comyn wished, that Scotland might be one;
But Comyn thought to get the crown by guile,
And weakly, wickedly betrayed his friend,
Setting between him and the English king
A gulf of enmity impassable.
Edward will judge him out of church and law;
But in our Scotch communion he is safe:
And being out of law, there is no way,
Except to be our King, above the law.
Needs must, my lords; and is not need God's will?

Edward Bruce. It is the will of God.

All.   Bruce shall be King.

(*Enter* BRUCE)

Long live the King!   Long live King Robert
  Bruce !

Bruce.   You hail me by a name that may be
  mine
In more than word, but not without your aid.
There are not many Scots besides yourselves
Who will acknowledge me their King.   Think
  well
Before you pledge your faith to one out-
  lawed ;
For so I am, if law depend on power.
Scotland, the Isles, and England are my
  foes :
My friends are individual ; on my hands
They may be counted.   Lennox, Athole,
  Cairns,
Fleming, the Hayes, the Frasers, Sommerville,
Glasgow, and Moray, sum the list with you :
These only are the Scots whom I may rule.

Sir Christopher Seton. Then only these deserve the name of Scot.

Lamberton. Right, Seton!

Randolf. We are Scots, the rest are slaves!
Freeman and Scot have ever meant the same.

Lamberton. Carrick or King?

Bruce. King, by God's will and yours.

Lamberton. Sometimes we please ourselves
 with images
Of deeds heroic. The unstabled thought,
Enfranchised by rough-riding passion, winds
A haughty course and laughs at depth and
 height:
But the blood tires; and lo! our thought, a
 steed,
That from his rider ever takes the mood,
Pants, droops, turns tail, and hobbles home
 to stall.
Look in yourselves, and see if vain conceit
Or lofty daring, lord it o'er your minds.

This thing is sure: reason must be constrained:
You must be hot, believing, fanatic;
You must be wrathful, patriotic, rash;
Forethought abandon o'er to providence;
Let prudence lag behind you, like a snail,
Bearing its house with care upon its back;
Take counsel only of the circumstance
That shapes itself in doing of the deed;
Be happy, scornful, death-defiant: strong
You will be then, matchless, invincible.
What! shall we go to Scone, and crown Bruce
    King?

Randolf. At once, Lord Archbishop.

Sir John Seton. To Glasgow, first,
To take our friends there with us.

Lamberton. That is best.
Is it your will to be crowned King at Scone?

Bruce. Most reverend father, and my noble
    friends,
If language were to me in place of thought,
I could pour grateful speeches in your ears;

But words are wanting. I am helpless, dumb;
I would be lonely; I would think awhile.

Lamberton.   Think worthy thoughts, that only second are
To worthy deeds; yet their begetters too.
We'll leave you till our little troop's arrayed.

Bruce.   You are very kind, my Lords.

[*Exeunt all except* BRUCE.

I'm not a man
Much given to meditate.   When pending thoughts
Hurtle each other in the intellect,
Darkening that firmament like thunder-clouds,
To let them lighten forth in utterance
Clears up the sky, confused with swaying rack.
My life begins a new departure here;
And like one dying all my time appears
Even on the instant, in eternal light.
Ambition struck the hours that measured it.
My pact with Comyn was half-hearted.   What!
The passion that laid hold upon my soul

When he was killed—When he was killed?
   I think
I'm to myself too merciful; but yet
I seemed to do some bidding:—were there
   not
Alloys of gladness that the bond was loosed,
Of jealousy that Comyn barred my way
Mixed in the blow that paid the traitor's
   wage?
There are two voices whispering in my ear.
This is the bane of self-communion. Now,
Right in thy teeth, or in thy toothless chaps,
I swear, antiquity, first thoughts are best:
Their treble notes I still shall hearken to,
And let no second, murmuring soft, seduce
Their clear and forthright meaning. It is
   gone,
The flash of revelation: dallying does
With intuition as with other chance.
I would to God that I might ever hear
The trump of doom pealing along the sky,
And know that every common neighbour day
Is the last day, and so live on and fight
In presence of the judgment. Wishing this

Have I not broached the very heart of truth?
Each unmarked moment is an end of time,
And this begins the future.

     [*Enter* ISABELLA.

      Isabella!

Isabella. What in this time of doleful accidents
Could move the joyful shouts I heard just now?

Bruce. My dearest, what would make you shout for joy?

Isabella. I have not shouted since I was a girl;
But now, I think, if any happy thing
Should spring into my life I would cry out,
I have been so unhappy, and so long.
Tell me you'll never leave me any more;
Then will I cry, and weep, for very joy.

Bruce. Heaven grant it may be so!

Isabella.   If there is hope !—
Did I not shout now?—I will nurse it warm,
And pet it like a darling, till it come
To be what I imagine in the fact,
Or in the fancy; for I will go mad:
I'll bend myself to lose all faculty,
All thought, remembrance, all intelligence,
So to be capable of company
With your phantasm, more real then than
  life;
And be a wild mad woman, if those fears,
Those weary absences, those partings pale,
And fevered expectations, which have filled
The summer of our life with storm and cold,
Determine not in peace and halcyon days.
You do not love me as I love you; no;
Else you would never leave me.   Love of
  power
And love of me hold tourney in your breast.
Let Will throw down the baton, and declare
The love of me the winner, and I'll be
Your queen of love; and beautiful as love
For man can make a woman.   I am proud:
When love transfigures me I can conceive

How beautiful I am. Stay with me, then,
That holy, sweet, and confident desire
May light me up a pleasant bower for you :
I am, when you are gone, a house forlorn,
Cold, desolate, and hasting to decay :
Stay, tenant me, preserve me in repair ;
Only sweet uses keep sweet beauty fair.

Bruce. I love you, Isabella, by high heaven,
More than the highest power that can be mine.

Isabella. Why then pursue this power so ardently ?

Bruce. I stayed pursuit ; but it would follow me.
My countrymen have asked me to be King.

Isabella. King !—But you murdered Comyn.
    All his friends—
Forgive me, love. I would not for the world
Reproach you ; but——

Bruce. I know your gentle heart.
My thought of you is not the morning bride;
Nor even the rose that oped its balmy breast
And gave its nectar sweetly. In my mind
This memory of you crowds out the rest:
The woman who with tender arms embraced
The bloody murderer. I know your heart.

Isabella. Hush!

Bruce. Friends are few; but if my title's
  good?
Hopeless the cause; but if the cause be just?
I'm glad my hand that did my passion's hest
Has made my mind up for me.

Isabella. You'll be king?

Bruce. Will I be hunted like a common
  knave
Who stabs his comrade in a drunken brawl
For some rude jest or ruder courtesan,
And, being an outlaw, dies by any hand?
I'd rather be the King; and though I die

The meanest death, be held in memory
As one who, having entered on a course
Of righteous warfare by a gate of shame,
Pursued it with his might, and made amends
For starting false—so far as lay in him;
For out of him his sin is, stablished, past,
And by a life's atonement unredeemed.
I do not brood on this.   Before you came
I had better thoughts.

Isabella.   O, I am sad at that!

Bruce.   I love you: not from you those worse
   thoughts sprang.

Isabella.   Perhaps they did: for I have some-
   times found,
When I have spent an hour in decking me,
But thinking more to please you in my life
Than in my dress, that, coming then to you,
Brimming with tenderness, some thoughtless
   word,
Or even a look from you has changed my
   mood,

And made me deem the world a wilderness;
While this cross glance, or inauspicious tone,
Was but a feint of yours, whose strength of
    love
Withheld itself, afraid it should undo
Its purpose by endeavouring too much:
And we have parted, discontented both.
But we'll not part now. Say, we shall not
    part.

Bruce. Not now. We will be crowned to-
    gether, queen.

Isabella. 'But then' succeeds 'not now;' I
    hope, far off.

Bruce. We must prepare to go.

Isabella. So soon!

Bruce. Our friends
Await us, chafing doubtless at delay.

Isabella. Then I will make a proverb lie for
    once,

And be on horseback sooner than my lord.
[*Exeunt.*

SCENE II.—*A Road in Dumfriesshire. Enter* BRUCE, ISABELLA, *and a* SQUIRE.

Bruce. Look to our horses while we rest.
[*Exit* SQUIRE.

Isabella. How far
Are we before our friends?

Bruce. See, they appear.

Isabella. That little puff of dust?

Bruce. Our company,
Three miles away I think. The road is straight,
And slopes to us. I hear a hoof—this side.

Isabella. It is a solitary knight, but one

Who need not fear to ride afar, alone,
If I may trust a woman's hasty eye.
He is dismounting ; he unhelms, he bows ;
He seems to know you, and salute you king !

Enter SIR JAMES DOUGLAS.

Bruce. Douglas ! I thought that Paris would retain
For years to come the service of your youth.

Douglas. You speak as one whom some transcending hap
Has shewn the high and secret worth of life ;
And such am I, or else discourtesy
Alone had greeted me in what you said.
Not with shrunk purse, drained veins, and heart dried-up ;
Will, broken-winded ; pith-brains ; sinews —straw,
From Paris, which unstiffens many a one,
Come I to Scotland, where is need of strength.
A love of noble things—a kind of faith—
A hope, a wish, a thought above the world,

Has swayed me from the mire; and yet I know
It is a miracle I'm not more soiled.

Bruce.   I spoke unworthily of this reply,
And gladly now unsay my hinted charge,
Which, with less thought than commonplace, I made;
Though I should utter nothing now but thought,
For as you judged I see a soul in life.
And what in Scotland do you think to do?

Douglas.   Retrieve my lands, avenge my father's death,
And drive the English from its borders. Here
I offer Scotland's king my lance, and here
I vow to be his lady's loyal knight.
You are amazed.   They say, ill news spreads fast:
He whom the tidings then will halcyon
Knows of his weal as soon as he his woe.
Is the news good to you that Bruce is king?

Bruce.   The news is good: best, that he's
    king of you.
I wonder most at that.   I stood in arms
Against your father, and but yesterday
I seemed the friend of England.

Douglas.   Yesterday
Was once the date of every lasting change.
While you are faithful to the land that's yours,
I swear to serve you faithfully till death.

Bruce.   Another trusty friend when friends
    are few—
And such a friend!   Welcome, a thousand
    times!

Isabella.   A happy handselling of our enter-
    prize!
What is the news from England?   Have you
    heard
If Wallace has been judged?

Douglas.   Not yet; but soon
In Westminster he will be doomed to death;

For victory, which oft ennobles kings,
Debases Edward. Since he has not grace,
The gracious-hearted world with one outcry
Should claim the life of Wallace for its own,
As the most noble life lived in this age,
And not to be cut off by one man's hate.

Bruce.   The thought of Wallace troubles me.
    The truth
That great men seldom in their times are
    known;
And this that little men are eminent
In midst of their thin lives and loud affairs,
Assert how perilous election is
By peers all bound and circumstanced alike.
If he were solely moved by noble thoughts,
And is the signal hero you give out—
Nothing I say, and nothing I deny—
Then were the nobles who deserted him
Unworthy cowards, beggars, churls, knaves,
    hounds.
Shall I condemn my order so ? or think
That Wallace hoped to aggrandize himself,

And lost those friends who had no need to
    fight
For mere existence when the restive hoof
Of personal ambition kicked aside
The patriot's caparison? You wince:
But with the time I drift, and cannot find
A mooring for my judgment. Pardon me.
This I believe: there is no warrior
Before the world, who could, even with those
    means
Of formal power that Wallace mostly lacked,
Have wrought the tithe of his accomplish-
    ment.
His name will be an ensign; and his acts
The inspiration of his countrymen.

Douglas. You yet will know his magna-
    nimity
Which girdled round the ample continent
Of his performance like the boundless sea.

Bruce. I'm glad to think—to know the best
    of him.
Shall we turn back and meet our friends?

Isabella. Yes; come.
And, Douglas, tell us more of Wallace, pray.

                            [*Exeunt.*

SCENE III.—*A Room in the* EARL OF BUCHAN'S *Castle. Enter the* EARL *and the* COUNTESS OF BUCHAN, *and the* EARL OF FIFE.

Countess of Buchan. Once more, I beg you, brother, on my knees,
To undertake the duty of your race.
Now, while I plead, they may be crowning him,
And no Macduff to gird his curling hair.
Eleven kings from Malcolm Canmore's time
Our ancestors have perfected with gold,
Laying the ruddy chaplet on their brows
Like magic dawn that tops the day with light.
It is a custom that has come to mean
The thing it garnished; and he cannot be
The King of Scots, however just his claim,

However consecrated, sceptred, throned,
Who is not crowned by you.

Fife.   I am the friend
Of England, of your husband; finally
Be answered I beseech you.   If you plead
Again with such hot vehemence, I'll think
Your husband is a fool to slight the word
That birds have carried of the Bruce and
   you.

Countess of Buchan.   If I were richer than
   to need your help,
I'd let you know that brother's quality
Who dares to doubt his mother's daughter.
   Shame!
But I am passionate, and so are you:
You meant no wrong.   You'll do this, will
   you not?

Fife.   Why! here's a woman! — What a
   woman!   Well!
I tell you I am England's friend, which means
The foe of any upstart such as Bruce;

And I am Buchan's friend, which means the
 foe
Of Buchan's mortal foe the outlaw Bruce.
I tell you this, and yet you beg of me
To do for Bruce the service needed most
To make him mighty in his enmity.

Countess of Buchan. If you were armed to
 fight a champion,
And he had lost his helm before you met,
You would not do despite to chivalry,
And take advantage of his naked head,
But find him in a morion, or unclasp
Your own, and equally defended, charge.
Be chivalrous to Bruce; make him a king
That Edward may be vantageless in that.
Then fight for Edward, with your puissance,
 fight.

Fife. I think you're mad. This pertinacity,
Which you intend shall urge me to comply—
Which you conceive no doubt a sign of
 strength,
But which I judge a sign of vanity—

Is one of women's weapons, well-approved,
With which she jags to death a stronger will.
But my resolve is harnessed, and your dart
Turns off it blunt—and spent, I hope.

Buchan. You hear;
I said you could not move him.—Come
    away.—
I'm sorry you have set your mind on this.

                [*Exeunt* FIFE *and* BUCHAN.

Countess of Buchan. To toss my hair, to
    weep, to rate my maid,
Are small reliefs I ne'er resorted to;
And now I must do something notable.
What if I went and crowned the Bruce myself?
Ah! here's a thought that's like a draught of
    wine!
My brother, whose the office is, resiles:
Mine—mine it is!—But how?—but if I did?
Their tongues, their tongues! their fou
    imaginings!
Is the world wicked as its thought is?—Love?
There's no one would believe me if I vowed

Upon my death-bed, between heaven and
    earth,
I understand no meaning in the word.
Maidens have lovers, and they sigh and wake;
Wives love their husbands, and they wake and
    weep :
But never, never have I loved a man,
As I see women love—with bursting hearts,
With fire and snow at variance in their cheeks,
With arching smiles, the heraldry of joy,
Whose rainbow shadows shine on hot hard
    tears ;
With cruel passion, dying ecstasy,
With rapture of the resurrection-morn.
I have not loved. It may be to my shame,
But justly to the world's, condemning me
For deeds no cause could work me to commit.
If I take horse to Scone, farewell my fame,
Which halts yet at the threshold.—Who's
    this ?
                [*Enter* JAMES CROMBE.
           Crombe !—
Do you remember in my father's house
Your life once stood in danger for a crime—

Which I'll not name—when mercy at my
  plea
Was meted you in place of punishment?

Crombe. · Well I remember.

Countess of Buchan. You were thankful
  then,
And held your life at my command. The
  time—

Crombe. My lady, if some service you
  require
Perilling my life, I'll do it willingly;
But had you urged my love, my duteous love;
And not my debt, I had been happier.

Countess of Buchan. I beg your pardon, sir.
  Indeed, I think
The service I require may cost your life,
But surely something dearer. I am whirled
From thought to thought: my mind lacks
  breath. Good Crombe,
You owe me nothing. Will you, if I bid,

Procure me black dishonour, and yourself
A name of loathing ?.

Crombe. No, my lady.

Countess of Buchan. How ?

Crombe. If I beheld you hurrying to your
  shame
I'd keep your honour holy with my sword,
And send it hot to heaven.

Countess of Buchan. Well.—You're a Scot ?
I mean, you long for Scotland's freedom.

Crombe. Yes.

Countess of Buchan. Are you acquainted
  with the news ?

Crombe. Of Bruce ?
I've heard they mean to crown him king to-
  day ;
But since my lord of Fife is England's friend—

Countess of Buchan.   Yes, yes! But are you
   glad?

Crombe.   Most heartily.
I think of joining Bruce.

Countess of Buchan.   My timorous heart,
Fie, fie!—I knew you were a noble man.
You will put no construction but the right
On what I mean to do.   Both you and I
Must be dishonoured in the world's regard:
I, an unfaithful wife; you, go-between.
Saddle two horses; lead them secretly
A mile beyond the castle.   There I'll mount,
And ride with you to Scone.   Go, instantly.
I, Isobel Macduff, will crown Bruce king.

Crombe.   But, noble lady—not for fear but
   safety—
What of pursuit?

Countess of Buchan.   Pursuit?   I am a mint,
And coin ideas.   Come—come out!   It's
   gold!

My husband's horses must be aired to-day.
You'll see it done. Some of the grooms we'll bribe,
And some will come unbought, and some we'll force
Either to follow us, or quit their steeds.
Leave nothing in the stables that can run.
My lords—ha, ha!—are nowhere in the chase.

Crombe. Captain, and countess, mistress, service-worthy,
Be confident in me, as I in you,
And the deed's done.
[Exit.

Countess of Buchan. Now world, wag, wag, your tongues!
I sacrifice my fame to make a king :
And he will raise this nation's head again
That lies so low ; and they will honour him ;
And afterwards, perhaps, they'll honour me.
Or if they slight me and my modest work,
I will be dead : I have enough to bear

Of disrespect and slander here to-day,
Without forecasting railing epitaphs.
But some—nay, many of the worthiest,
And many simple judgments too, will see
The sunlight on my deed. This, I make
    sure ;
No Scot's allegiance can be held from Bruce
Because he was not crowned by a Macduff.—
And if I love him, what is that to him ?
That's a good saying. So is this, I make :
If I do love him, what is that to me !
                              [*Exit.*

ACT III.

SCENE I.—WESTMINSTER. *The Hall of the Palace.* KING EDWARD I. *on a throne of state. In attendance, lords* PEMBROKE, PERCY, CLIFFORD, *and other lords, gentlemen, and officers. Enter* SIR PETER MALLORIE *with* SIR WILLIAM WALLACE, *bound and guarded.*

Edward I. Proceed with the impeachment, Mallorie.

Mallorie. Sir William Wallace, knight of Elderslie,
Some time usurping Guardian of Scotland,
You are a traitor to the English crown—

Wallace. I am no traitor to the English crown,
For I was never subject to King Edward.

Mallorie. Therein your treason rests. But speak not now:
You may speak afterwards in your defence.

Wallace. I will speak now, not to excuse my deeds,
But to arraign the falsest traitor here.
Edward of England, if one pure pulse beats
In that debauched and enervated core,
Which was your conscience, I will make it ache.

Edward I. What do you mean? To have us think you mad,
And to your frailty that compassion show,
Which crimes and sins forbid us to extend?
Or are you posing as a prodigy
Of heroism? In their minstrelsy
They sing of captive knights whose bold address
In presence of their victors won them grace:
But know that justice sees no worth in words—
Deeds only: therefore hear your deeds rehearsed.

Mallorie.   Sir William Wallace, treasons
    manifold—

Wallace.   I crave the pardon of all manhood
    here.
Having small use for any faculty
Since I became a captive, I have slacked
The rigour of my will, and thus it is
I spoke with petulance before my time.
Proceed to read my accusation, sir.

Mallorie.   You are accused of many treason-
    ous acts
Done on the persons, castles, cities, lands,
Of our most noble sovereign, Edward First,
In England and in Scotland—

Wallace.   But, explain—

Edward I.   Silence, guilty felon!

Wallace.   Guilty?   Condemned,
And hanged already, doubtless, in your heart.
I will confess my guilt, for I am guilty.—

Guilty of failure in a righteous cause.
I will confess that when ill-fortune came
My friends forsook me; that I lost the day
At Falkirk, and have since been little worth.
I stayed your accusation, sir, to ask
What treason I could work against a king
Whom I acknowledge not, and in a land
Not governed by that king?

Edward I.   Silence!—Proceed.

Wallace.   What! English Edward! Would you roar me down?
My deeds have spoken: shall I fear your tongue?
The charge against me is irrelevant;
No jurisdiction have you over me
To pardon or to doom: prisoner of war,
No traitor, I; and here I make demand
For knightly treatment at the hands of knights.

Edward I.   You shall have justice.

Wallace. In the end I shall:
And so shall you. Death you have often
 faced;
Justice you shall see once.

Edward I. Stay, Mallorie.
We'll tutor this heroic insolence.—
The observant world has notched the life of
 man,
And three main periods indicate three powers
Whose dreadful might directs our very stars.
These powers take reason's throne, the
 intellect.
First, love usurps, like Saturn come again—
Whose orb is yet man's most malignant foe—
Turning the sad, outlandish time of youth
Into a golden age. Ambition rules
With godly sway the second period,
And marshals man's capacity to war
Against the evils that beset him most,
And win what things of worship he desires.
Prudence, which none but old men under-
 stand
To be the strongest tyrant of the three,

Reigns lastly, making peace with God and
    man;
Securing acquisitions; peering forth
Into the future, like a mariner,
Whose freight is landed in a foreign port,
With wistful homeward gaze, but eager yet
To see his merchandize disposed of well.
And reason, which should rule, most cheer-
    fully
Accepts the ministry beneath these kings.
This is the chronicle of noble men.
The sun gleams lurid through a rotting fog,
And those pure powers that shine in lucent
    souls,
Clear, as if lanterned only by the air,
In natures base, burn with a murky flame,
As lust, concupiscence, and avarice:
And reason, mad with degradation, toils
Unwillingly in slavish offices.
Now comes my application. Cruel, vain,
Intolerant, unjust, false, murderous,
You, Wallace—rebel, outlaw, hangman, fool,
Incendiary, reiver, ravisher—
You are the serf of vile concupiscence—

Yea, of the vilest famine—hungry greed
Of notoriety!—the commonest,
The meanest, lewdest, gauntest appetite,
That drives the ignoble to extremity!
No sooner had we quarried painfully,
Forth of that chaos left by your King John,
A corner-stone for righteous government,
Than you and other itching malcontents
With gothic hands o'erturned the fane of
    peace,
And on your groaning land brought heathen
    war,
That you might win the name of patriot.
Again I built up order; and again
You overthrew my government, and caused
Your fatherland—heroic patriot!—
From Tweed to Moray Frith to swim in
    blood,
Before divine authority could rule.
Still you rebelled; for you must stand
    alone—
And think not, lords, I over-rate the strength
Of this delirious thirst for some repute—

Though nobles, knights, burgesses, yeomen,
  priests,
Yea, every Scot, well-pleased, acknowledged
  us,
You—cast-off guardian—dog that had his
  day—
Alone, unfriended, starving in the wilds,
Held there aloof, and signalized your night
By howling for that moon you almost
  clutched,
A tyrant's power, calling it liberty :
For that was still behind your lust of fame.

Mallorie.   You're silent now.

A Lord.   Silence becomes him well.
This just exposure stills his shameful voice.

Wallace.   Seeing how your rage leapt from
  your lips in lies,
King, I bethink me ere I make reply,
Lest I, too, throw the truth.

Edward I.   Now tell us, lords,

Are we on our defence or Wallace? which?
Villain, regard law's form if not its soul.
Be better mannered; touch your memory;
You stand before the majesty of England.

Wallace. I stand there truly; but behind
    me pants
The king of terrors; and his quiver holds
One dart I hope to parry, which I fear—
But not the venomed shaft that nothing
    fends.
It is—not now; I'll tell you afterwards.—
Noble?—ignoble?—who shall judge us, king?
This deed and that we may with help of
    heaven
Christen or damn, and not be far astray;
But who shall take upon him to declare
The mind of God on what is unrevealed,
The guiding thought, deep, secret, which is
    known,
Even to the thinker, but in passing wafts.
Because my life was spent in thwarting you,
I am not therefore an incarnate fiend,
Although the justice of the end I stayed

Possessed your soul to sickening. Mad for
 fame ! —
My wife's, my father's, and my brothers'
 deaths—

Edward I. No more of this. Call in the
 witnesses.

Wallace. I'll speak now, and be heard.

All. Silence ! Be still.

Wallace. I can outroar you all. Sound
 trumpets, drums,
And fill your hall with clamour, I shall speak,
And you shall hear. Above the voice of war
I have been heard, and—

All. Silence, traitor, silence !

[*The shouting continues for a little, but gradually ceases as* WALLACE *speaks on.*

Wallace. I fought for liberty and not for
 fame.

Monarchs know not the inestimable worth
Of that imperial, rich diadem
Which only crowns both kings and carls, men.
Say, slavery unfelt were possible,
Then freedom is a name for sounding wind.
But call me slave in any mincing term;
And let the tyrant's frowns be smiles of love;
The chains, less galling than a lady's arms;
The labour, just my pleasure's ministry:
If I surrender to the conqueror,
As captive is my soul, as though thick irons
Wore through my flesh, and rusting in my
 blood,
Rasped on my bones, the while with lash and
 oath
Some vicious tasker held me to hard toil.
I stand here free, though bound and doomed
 to die.
And know, King Edward, every Scot, who
 bent,
Gnawing his heart, a recreant knee to you,
Perjured himself, being free; and even now—
I know my countrymen—contrite they rise;
And when they have another leader—one,

Abler than I—pray heaven, more fortunate!—
They will anew throw off your galling yoke,
And be, once more, lieges of liberty.
I am the heart of Scotland; when I die
It shall take heart again—

Edward I.   No, no! by heaven!
The Scots repudiate you!

Wallace.   The Scots do not :
The people, pulse for pulse, beat warm with
　　me.

Edward I.   You lie! You lie!—But I forget
　　myself.
Freebooters, prodigals, scroyles — outcasts
　　all—
Your sole supporters, may lament your end;
But true men everywhere are jubilant.
Not England only, and the better part
Of your divided country were your foes ;
But from the world's beginning you were
　　doomed
To fail in your unholy enterprize.

For destiny, whose servant nature is,
Ordained by the creation of this land—
So long sore vexed by chance, fate's enemy,
With heptarchies, divisions, kings and clans—
That one king and one people here should
    dwell,
Clasped in the sea's embrace, happy and safe
As heaven is, anchored in eternity.
In fighting me you fought fate's champion,
Anointed with the fitness of the time,
And with the strength of his desire inspired,
To finish nature's work in Albion.
You, paltry minion of a band of knaves,
In name of patriotism—which in this case
Was in the devil's name—fought against God;
The coming of His kingdom hindered here.
Now His sure vengeance has o'ertaken you,
And over both our lands His sweet peace
    reigns.

Wallace.   Eternal God, record this blas-
    phemy!
Who doubts our lands are destined to be one?
Who does not pray for that accomplishment?

Why!   Know you not that is the period,
The ultimate effect I battled for,
That you, free English, and that we, free Scots,
May one day be free Britons.   And we shall;
For Scotland never will be tributary:
We are your equals, not to be enslaved;
We are your kin, your brothers, to be loved.
Time is not ripe: fate's crescent purposes,
Like aloe-trees, bloom not by forcing them;
But seasonable changes, mellowing years,
Elaborative ages, must mature
The destined blossoms.   Listen, king and lords;
Here is a thing worthy remembering,
And which perhaps you never rightly knew:
Duty is always to the owner done;
And the immediate debtor wisely pays:
The heritage of duty unperformed
Increases out of sight of usury.
Restore to Scotland freedom.   Do that, king,
Or it will be required from you or yours
With woeful interest.—I have done.   I feared

I might not find a way to speak these truths,
Having no nimble tongue, and die oppressed
With warning unpronounced. I truly thought
I could command a hearing had I words.
Death now, the due of all, my triumph, waits.

Edward I. (*coughing.*) The witnesses, Sir Peter Mallorie;
Your accusation now is needless.

Mallorie. Sire,
Hugh Beaumont is the first. He'll testify
Of early deeds in the arch-traitor's life.
He is an old man now and garrulous:
A gentleman withal, whose gentle blood
Stood him in little stead, when windy youth
Had sown itself, and whirling poverty
Down to the barren common dashed his head.
So with his sword he battened as he might,
And valour was his star. Let him have scope,
For he has much to say.

[HUGH BEAUMONT *is led in.*

       Inform the king
As strictly as to God of all that passed
Between you and the prisoner.

Edward I. Speak the truth.

Beaumont. Your gracious majesty, what I
  can tell
Is liker fable; but the noble knight,
The prisoner, will acknowledge all I say:
Much of it honours him.—To Ayr he came
One day, disguised, with hat down, cloak
  pulled up.

There as he paced the street, Lord Percy's
  man
Seized on some fish a burgher just had
  bought;
Whereat, Sir William, like a smouldering fire,
Flared up to burn the foot whose thoughtless
  kick
Had tortured it to flame. In speechless rage

He grasped the caitiff's throat and smote him
    dead.
About two score well harnessed Englishmen,
With whom I was, did straight environ him.
Against a wall he bore which seemed to be
Rather upheld by him than him unholding,
And reaped us down like corn. He did, my
    lords.
He multiplied his strokes so that he seemed
To multiply himself; there did appear
Opposed to every soldier there, a Wallace.
Without or helm or mail, in summer-weed,
Grass-green, flowered red with blood, he
    fought us all,
Till one that bit the dust writhed near enough
To pierce him in the leg and then he fell.
Yet even so he might have won away;
But as he rose he fetched a blow at me,
Which I eluding, down his breaking brand
Upon the causeway struck; and in his eyes
A light went out, when his up-lifted hand
Showed but the hilt. In faith I pitied him.
I pitied him, and bore him to the tower.
There in a filthy dungeon he expired

Of festering wounds and food that swine refused,
Ere they had settled what death was his due.

Edward I.   But he is here alive?

Beaumont.   Pardon, dread lord;
He seemed at that time dead: the West mourned for him:
His aged nurse bought his corrupting corpse
To bury it decently in hallowed ground.—
Well, after that a while, in Lanark-town,
I waited in the High Street on the judge,
Lord Ormesby, then on circuit in the west.
Four men were with me.   One, on fire with wine,
A braggart at the best, vaunted his deeds.
And when two men came down the street, he cried,
"See yonder stalks a canny muffled Scot,
A strapper, by this light! attended, too!
He's like to have that may be taxable.
Something I'll mulct him of; or something give,

That shall be worse than nothing, namely
    blows!"
"Belike," said I, "that boon will not go quit.
His side is guarded by a lengthy purse,
Whose bright contents, I think, he will not
    hoard."
"I'll have his sword," quoth he, "If he refuse,
Take it, and beat him with it, till he shake
His dastard body out of his habergeon;
Which, leaving here, he'll give me hearty
    thanks,
That I leave him his skin, the lousy Scot!"
And so he staggered out to meet the two.
The muffled stranger whispered to his man,
And he sped on before in anxious haste,
Dodging the drunk man's outstretched arm,
Who said, "Well, you may go; your master
    is behind."
And when the master came he stopped him,
    saying,
"Knave Scot, unveil! Come, show your
    sonsy face.
Vile thief, where did you steal this tabard
    green?

And where the devil got you this fair knife?
What! jewelled in the hilt! Unbuckle, quick,
Mantle and whittle; and to make amends
For having ever worn them clasp them both
About me, and you shall have leave to go."
"St. Andrew! There's my whittle, English
    dog!"
And with a thrust the Scot let out his life.
We others rushed upon him instantly,
Shouting, "Down with him! Vengeance on
    the Scot!"
He gave us back, "St. Andrew, and the right!"
Wrapping his arm in what had wrapped his
    face,
And looking like the lion that he was.
Beholding him I trembled, and stood still;
But one more rash ran on, to shriek and fall,
His raised right arm lopped at the shoulder
    off.
With that a voice cried, "In the king's name,
    peace!"
The Scot looked up and saw a troop approach.
"Too great a pack for one," he said, and ran.
Now this was Ormesby, the justiciary,

Arrived in Lanark to dispense the law,
With Hazelrig, the ruler of the shire.

Mallorie. (aside to Beaumont).   Quick man!
    be quick! Look how his highness chafes!

Beaumont.   The valiant Scot was Wallace.
    It appeared
His foster-mother, who had paid away
The earnings of her lifetime for his corpse,
Kissing, and weeping o'er it, saw a spark
Struggle with night of death; or else her
    hope
Inspired new breath, much aided by her
    prayers.
The little glow she nursed into a flame,
So feeble, that, lest meat should smother it,
Her daughter gave one of her bosom's
    springs,
Then at high-tide to feed her new-born babe,
For the replenishing his body's lamp.
Being recovered, he had come to see
His wife, who dwelt in Lanark.

Wallace. *(aside).* God ! O God !

Beaumont. Hazelrig led the chase. I followed close.
We reached the house. I searched the garden. There,
Scarcely concealed, I saw the prisoner. Sire,
I'm not a coward, and I was not then ;
But from the instant that I recognised
The dead man come alive, enchantment caught
My spirit in a toil, and made me watch
Powerless and voiceless, all he did. I felt
No movement, even while I followed him.
There was some witchery I do believe.
In by the window when the search was o'er,
He entered, saying gaily to his wife,
"I almost think an English lourdane saw me.
How thin a thicket hides a dread discovery !"
Then seeing on the floor his lady lie,
"O God ! what varied truth was in that word !
Not dead, my love !" She spoke that I could hear.

"Dying, dying. Hazelrig has killed me
My spirit clings still to my lips to kiss you.
I would my soul might melt into a kiss
To lie on your lips till your soul's release,
And then to heaven together we would fly.
Avenge my death and Scotland's wrongs."
    "My love!"
He cried; and all his strength was water.
And long he held her: and he shook and
    sobbed.

Wallace. (straining his bonds.) Nay, hang
    me!—burn me!—I am sawn asunder!

Beaumont. At length he put her softly on a
    seat,
And took her hand, and knelt: and she was
    dead.
Her face was like an angel's fallen asleep.
Upon her bloody breast his eyes he fixed,
Seeming unruffled as a still white flame,
And words, more dread than silence, spake
    aloud.

"I will avenge thy death and Scotland's
    wrongs.
For every tear that now my eyes have dropped
From English veins shall seas of blood be
    shed.
Each sigh of mine shall have ten thousand
    echoes :
Yea, for her death, I'll England sepulchre.
O, glutton grave, a surfeit shall be thine!
Death's self shall sleep before my vengeance
    flags."
Slowly retiring with his face to her
He went. I have not seen him since till now.
He was a young man then.

                      [*Voices within.*

Edward I. What noise is that?

Clifford. A messenger, my lord, would force
    the door.

Edward I. Whence comes he?

Clifford. From the north, your majesty.

Edward I.   Admit him.

(*Enter* MESSENGER.)

Welcome, sir.   Your news at once,
Plainly and nakedly.

Messenger.   Comyn is dead :
Slain in Dumfries by Bruce; whose party then,
Led by the fiery Edward, mad as he,
Attacked and seized the castle.   On the day
I left the north, in Scone, the Lady Buchan,
The Bruce's paramour, Fife's sister, crowned
Her murderous lover king.   Some lords and knights
Have gathered round him, and he lies at Perth.

Edward I.   Besotted fool!   But it is well.   Herein
I see God's hand hardening the heart of Bruce
Against me, who am but God's minister,
That I may cut him off.   I give God thanks.
Wallace—What! has he swooned?

Mallorie.   He's in a trance.
Wallace!—Well, this is strange!—Wallace!

Wallace. (*starting*).   My lords!

Edward I.   We'll countenance this mockery
   no more.
All England and all Scotland—all the world
Prejudge your fate.   Wherefore we will not
   then
Waste time in tedious processes of law
To find you, as we know you, dyed in guilt,
And leave another to pursue unchecked
A course of similar iniquity.
You for your treason are condemned to die
The death that traitors merit.   Lead him
   hence.
Come after me, my lords, immediately,
And take your charges for the north.

[*Exit* EDWARD I. *attended.* WALLACE
   *is led away.   As they go out they
   regard each other fixedly.*

Clifford. I think
The king but whiled the time with Wallace
  here,
Till news should come from Scotland.

Pembroke. With what haste
He sentenced him!

Percy. Yes; as a gamesome cat
Diverted with a mouse, scenting another,
Gobbles the captive quick.
                              [*Exeunt.*

ACT IV.

SCENE I.—*A Room in the* EARL OF BUCHAN'S *Castle. Enter the* EARL OF BUCHAN.

Buchan. This is not jealousy. I only ache
With sorrow that my trust has been reposed
In falseness; and I feel—I fear I feel
The whole world's finger quivering with scorn,
Stream venom at me. If I cannot sleep,
It is no wonder, for the laugh I hear,
Like icy water rippling—cold and true
As tested steel—so wise, so absolute,—
Is learned from those that know me by the fiend
Who watches with me nightly. Jealousy?
If it possessed me, mortal sickness, bonds,
Nothing in heaven or hell, would hold me back

From sating it with blood—with hers and
    his.
But I will not be jealous, like poor souls,
Whose vanity engrosses every thought,
And calls itself nobility; not I.
I will devise some vengeance, some just
    means,
Some condign punishment, the world will
    praise,
Thinking of me more highly than before
This miserable time.

Enter FIFE.

Fife. Brooding again !
Pluck up some sprightliness, for I have news.
Pembroke has routed Bruce in Methven
    wood,
And captured many leading rebels. Bruce,
Who showed himself a gallant warrior,
Proved in retreat wise as a veteran,
Escaping to the north.

Buchan. My wife?

Fife. They say
That she and other ladies northward too
In Nigel Bruce's charge escaped with speed.

Buchan. And is this sure?

Fife. I well believe it. Come,
Question the man who told me.

Buchan. If it's true
We'll join our powers and hunt the rebels down
Like noxious vermin, as they are.

Fife. Be cool.
What means this bitter passion?

Buchan. Am I hot?
But you'll combine with me?

Fife. Assuredly:
It is a noble chase; the quarry, game
To wind us over Scotland. Tally-ho!

Buchan. Now you are thoughtless. Come,
    the messenger.
[*Exeunt.*

SCENE II.—THE WOOD OF DROME. *Scotch soldiers about a watch-fire.*

1st Soldier. What clouted loons we are! Royal beadsmen! Eh?

2nd Soldier. The king's as ragged as the rest.

1st Soldier. That's true.
To-day I hunted with him, and I thought,
Seeing his doublet, loop-holed, frayed and fringed;
His swaddled legs, and home-made shoes of pelt;
His barbarous beard and hair, and freckled face,
That manhood's surely more than royalty;
For through this weedy, nettle-grown decay,
A majesty appeared that distanced us,
Even as a ruined palace overbears
A hamlet's desolation.

Enter BRUCE, *unperceived*

3rd Soldier.   He's a king
By nature; through descent we're lost in
    churls.

2nd Soldier.   Ay, ay; but mark : I'll reason
    of our state.
Here many days we've wasted in the wild,
Chased by the English like the deer we chase,
Exposed like them, without their native wont,
Beneath this fickle, rigorous northern clime,
Ill-fed, ill-clad, and excommunicate;
While decent burghers—Scots as true as we—
Live warm, and prosper with their families.
I think we're fools.

1st Soldier.   Fools for ourselves, maybe,
But wise I hope for Scotland : and the folk
In every town and village think us wise,
And bless and pray for us.

Bruce. (*aside*).   A brave heart that—
(*Advancing*) Good evening, comrades.   Can
    you guess the time ?

1st Soldier. An hour past sunset. Look, your
    majesty;
Barred by these trunks the cloudy embers
    burn
Where day is going out.

Bruce. Faintly I see.
Your fire's so bright it dims the distant glow.
Sit down again, good friends.

1st Soldier. A story, sir?

2nd Soldier. O, pray you tell us one!

Bruce. I think I will.
I've told you many tales of chivalry,
Of faerie, and of Greeks and Romans, too;
But now I'll tell you of a Scotchman, one
Who lived when Rôme was most puissant
    here.
The Roman governor, a valiant man,
Agricola, in whom ambition paused
Whenever prudence thought the utmost done,
Reconquered all the southern British tribes,
And drove his enemy beyond the Forth.

The noble Galgacus then swayed the realm
That stretches northward of that winding
    stream ;
And while the Roman, building forts and
    walls,
As was his wont, secured the bird in hand,
He mustered from his glens a skin-clad host
To fight for freedom.   Ardoch, they call it,
Where the armies met.   Ere the battle joined,
Firm on his chariot-floor with voice a-flame,
The Scottish chief harangued his thirty
    thousand.
"Brothers," he cried, "behold your enemies!
Gauls, Germans, Britons—mercenaries, slaves!
In conquest, one and strong ; but in defeat,
So many weaklings, heartless, hopeless, lost.
One signal victory to us were more
Than all the battles that our foes have won :
Their confidence is in their leader ; ours,
In our cause.   Hearken !—Had I a voice,
Like heaven's thunder, I would shout across
This battle-field to be, to yon mixed throng,
And tell them they are Britons, Germans,
    Gauls :

Bid them remember how in haughty Rome
Their free-born countrymén are taught to
    serve
The wanton fancies of luxurious vice
In perfumed chambers or in bloody shows;
Think of their wives and daughters, all
    abused;
Think of themselves, leagued with their con-
    querors
Armed and opposed against consanguine folk,
Placed in the van to bear the battle's brunt,
That Rome may triumph, and her blood not
    shed :
Then would they turn and rend with us the
    foe.
What need has Rome of Britain? we, of
    Rome?
We, the last lonely people of the north,
A morsel merely, perilous and far,
Incite the eagle appetite of Rome,
Uncloyed until she gorges all the world.
No other need has Rome. Poor, desolate,
Shrouded with mists, with cold empanoplied,
At war among ourselves, fighting with beasts,

We yet are freemen; and we need not Rome:
We are the only freemen in the world.
Here, in the very bosom of our land—
The last land in the world—we meet the power
That rules all other lands but ours. Even here
Let Rome be stricken. Brothers, countrymen,
Freedom has taken refuge in our hills.
She has a home upon the streaming seas,
But loves the land where men are hers. Let not
The word go forth on woeful-sounding winds
That Rome has driven freedom from the earth :
Sprite you with lions' hearts; like baleful stars
Inflame your eyes that their disastrous glance
May palsy foes afar; pour your whole strength
In every blow, nor fear a drought : the power
Of each is great as all when all are one.
Rush like a torrent ; crash like rocks that fall

When thunder rends the Grampians.
    Liberty!
Shatter the Romans, grind them, whelm
    them! Charge!"
The Scots were worthy of their gallant chief,
And fought as if they loved death, courting
    her
By daring her to opportunities;
Which she—a maid o'er-wooed—resented oft,
And strained their cooler rivals to her breast;
But discipline—that rock that bears the
    world,
Compactly built—a city on a cliff
Breaking disorder back like unknit waves—
Founded the Roman power; and on its
    front
The Scots beat, shivered by their own outset;
And evening saw them ebb, calmed, vanquished, spent.
Yet that lost battle was a gain: our hills,
That battle, and the ruin of her fleet,
Held Rome behind Grahame's dyke, and
    kept us Scots.
All south of us the Romans, Saxons, Danes,

And Normans, conquering in turn, o'erthrew
From change to change; but we are what we were
Before Aeneas came to Italy,
Free Scots; and though this great Plantagenet
Seems now triumphant, we will break his power.
Shall we not, comrades?

1st Soldier. Yes, your majesty.

2nd Soldier. But might it not have been a benefit
If Rome had conquered Scotland too, and made
Between the Orkneys and the Channel Isles
One nation?

Bruce. A subtle question, soldier;
But profitless, requiring fate unwound.
It might be well were all the world at peace,
One commonwealth, or governed by one king;

It might be paradise; but on the earth
You will not find a race so provident
As to be slaves to benefit their heirs.

1st Soldier.   At least we will not.

Bruce.   By St. Andrew, no !

(*Enter* NIGEL BRUCE).

My brother Nigel !   Happy and amazed
I see you here.   Why left you Aberdeen ?

Nigel.   For several ends.   And firstly, I
have news.

Bruce.   Come to our cave.

Nigel.   No ; for a reason, no.

Bruce.   Mysteries, secrets !—Well ; retire
good friends.
[*Exeunt soldiers.*

Nigel.   Perhaps my news is stale.

Bruce. Little I know
Since in the flight from Methven, panic-
  struck
We parted company.

Nigel. Learn then that Haye—
Hugh de la Haye; John is with you, I know—
Inchmartin, Fraser, Berclay, Somerville,
Young Randolf, Wishart, trusty Lamberton
Are captives.

Bruce. Half my world! But is it true?

Nigel. So much is certainty. Rumour
  declares
Young Randolf has deserted us; that those
I named will ransom; but that some,
  unknown,
Have died the death of traitors.

Bruce. Noble souls!
Randolf—poor boy! What more?

Nigel. A price
Is on your head.

Bruce.   That matters not.

Nigel.   I know.
Still have great heed of whom and how you
   trust.
That's all the evil tidings.   Hear the good.
The queen—Ah, this is she!   I'll leave you
   now.

Enter ISABELLA.

Bruce.   My dearest!

Isabella.   I couldn't wait, my husband.
The lady Douglas and the lady Buchan
Are in your cave.   We rode from Aberdeen
This evening, learning you were cantoned
   here.
Douglas was sleeping when we came.   His
   wife
Bent o'er him, and she slipped into his
   dream;
For when he waked he wondered not at all
To see his lady there, till memory

Aroused him quite to find the vision true.
Nigel was seeking you; but when I saw
The joy these two partook, incontinent
I hurried out myself to find like cheer.
My dear way-faring hero, I have come
To share your crust, and rags, and greenwood
    couch :
I'm deep in love with skied pavilions :
I'll be your shepherdess, Arcadian king.
This evening's journey lay throughout a
    wood :
The honeysuckle incensed all the air,
And cushats cooed in every fragrant fir;
Tall foxgloves nodded round the portly trees,
Like ruffling pages in the trains of knights;
Above the wood sometimes a green hill
    peered,
As if dame nature on her pillow turned
And showed a naked shoulder; all the way,
Whispering along, rose-bushes blushed like
    girls
That pass blood-stirring secrets fearfully,
Attending on a princess in her walk;
I think with rarely scented breath they said

A loving wife was speeding to her lord.
Why are you silent?

Bruce. I am thinking, dear,
That I'm the richest monarch in the world.
Possessing such a universe of love,
The treasure most desired by kings and clowns.

Isabella. What universe, dear lord?

Bruce. Simplicity!
How it becomes you! Gentle hypocrite,
You are my universe of love, you know.

Isabella. Then keep your universe, and do not waste
In empty space the time. I'll stay with you;
Surely I can? Come tell me all your plans.

Bruce. I've none. What I desire I know; and think
Firmly and honestly my wish is right.
Plans are for gods and rich men : I am poor.

Isabella. In spirit ? So you may be blame-
　　lessly ;
But are you, sir ?

Bruce. I hardly know. Just now
I tried to cheer a whining fellow here,
But stood myself in greater need of hope.

Isabella. I know—I understand. You need
　　to think
Of other things, my dear. I've heard of men,
Great men, exhausted even to lunacy
By just those labours that were beating
　　smooth
A thoroughfare for ever to success,
Repair themselves with youth's prerogative
That stops time and the world deposes, all
In favour of a dream ; or spend a while
With children or the simplest souls they
　　knew.
Come, you must be amused. But, tell me,
　　sir,
Am I to stay ?

Bruce. Yes, dearest pilgrim, yes.

Isabella. O, I am happy! We will live like
    birds.

Bruce. And in the winter?

Isabella. Winter? What is it?
This is the summer.

Bruce. Winter is—

Isabella. Hush!—hark!
What birds so late fly screaming overhead?

Bruce. Stout capercailzies, hurrying to their
    nests,
Sated with fir-tops.

Isabella. Ah! But, dearest lord
Are you quite well? I haven't asked you yet.

Bruce. I am very well. And you?

Isabella. See—look at me:
You used to know by gazing in my eyes.

Bruce. My wife, my lover, you are well indeed.

Isabella. The fire is nearly out. Come to the cave,
And there we will devise amusements, dear.

[*Exeunt.*

Scene III.—*Another Part of the* Wood of Drome. *The* Earl of Buchan *alone.*

Buchan. God help me and all jealous fools, I pray !
The plagues of Hades leagued in one raw scourge
Might minister diversion to my soul,
Assailing through my flesh. No thought at all
Of starry space or void eternity ;
Nor love, nor hate, nor vengeance, nor remorse—

My cousin's murder!—I've forgotten it!—
No sound of horns crackling with riotous
  breath
The crisp, rathe air; no hounds; no beckoning
  tunes
With notes of fiery down; nor singing girls
Whose voices brood and bound; nor chanting
  larks,
Nor hymning nightingales can touch my soul.
Nothing but torture unendurable
Wrought in the flesh has power on jealousy.
Slay him with agonies? A passing swoon!
I'll kill my wife!
Her blood is Lethe if oblivion be
Save in more high-strung anguish of my own.

Enter FIFE.

Fife. What is it? You have news.

Buchan. They are together—
The outlaw and your sister. They're at hand—
Three miles away—no more. A trusty spy
Told me just now.

Fife. Is there a band?

Buchan. Some score.

Fife. Then we will take them.

Buchan. Yes.

Fife. About it straight.
[*Exit.*

Buchan. I'll follow—Ho!

(*Enter* SPY.)

I thought you still were near.
I haven't thanked you yet. (*Gives money.*)
How did she look?
Was there about her not a thievish air,
A truant aspect, frightened and yet free,
Shame-faced, but bold, and like an angel lost.

Spy. Who, my good lord?

Re-enter FIFE.

Buchan. The queen—the outlaw's wife.

Spy. O no, my lord! She laughed, as she
    rode past
Where I lay hid, at something gaily said
By my good lady, your good lordship's wife.
They both looked happy riding in the sun.

Buchan. Aye; that will do.
                                  [*Exit* Spy.
                  I'm coming, Fife.

Fife. Stay yet.
You've not deceived me; and that fellow
    knows—
A side-look told me—that you tried and failed.
You meant my sister when you questioned
    him.
Tell me, what makes your jealousy so strong?
You never were in love with her I think.

Buchan. Nor am not now. I think—I
    know—I feel
What I have heard: true love is never jealous.
I am like other men; I love myself.
I cannot speak. I mean to act. Come on.
                                      [*Exeunt.*

Scene IV.—*A Cave in the* Wood of Drome, *with a fire at the back.* Bruce, Edward, *and* Nigel Bruce, Douglas, Crombe, Isabella, Countess of Buchan, Lady Douglas, *and others.*

Bruce. Who would build palaces when homes like these
Our kingdom yields us bosomed in her hills !
What tapestry, where the gloss and colour fade
From some love-story, overtold and stale,
Or where a famed old battle stagnates dim,
Befits a room before these unhewn walls
Whose shifting pictures lower and shine and live,
Ruddy and dark in leaping of the fire.
No homely mice in cupboards cheep ; the night
Is here not soothed by any mellow chirp
Of crickets, happily, devoutly busy ;
But in the ivy and the hollow oak

The owl has heard and learnt through day-
    long dreams
The wind's high note when pines in ranks are
    blown,
Bent, rent, and scattered with their roots in
    air,
And sounds his echo loud and dwindling
    long,
Fearfully as he flutters past our door;
The wild-cat screams far off in the pheasant's
    nest;
The werwolf, ravening in the warren, growls.
Night is no gossip here, watching the world
Sick-tired, heart-sore, sleep weariness away;
But free and noble, full of fantasy,
Queen of the earth, earth-bound, ethereal.

Isabella. (*aside*). His spirit rises. We must
    hold it up.—
My lord, shall lady Douglas sing?

Bruce. She shall.
Lady, I beg you sing us something sweet.
No trumpet notes, no war—

[1st *Soldier appears at the entrance of the cave.* DOUGLAS *whispers with him.*

What does he want?

Douglas. He comes as spokesman for his fellows.

Bruce. Well?

1st *Soldier.* (*advancing.*) I hope your highness will be patient with me.
My mates have bade me ask a favour, strange
And difficult to ask; but not so strange
If it be thought of well, nor difficult
If I can keep my head.

Bruce. Go on.

1st. *Soldier.* My lord,
For this great while we have seen no woman's face,
My mates and I: your highness knows that well.
When we beheld these ladies enter here,

A longing seized us all to look on them;
To see their faces and their gentle shapes;
And even to have them turn their eyes on us;
Perhaps to hear them speak. We are true men,
And honest in our thought.

Bruce. Bring them all in.

[*Exit 1st Soldier.*

Countess of Buchan. I know the mood that holds these men: brave lads!
If they were wed to women worth their love,
They would be nobler heroes than they are.

Isabella. We'll speak to them.

Countess of Buchan. I'll kiss that knave who spoke.

Lady Douglas. Will you?

Countess of Buchan. Yes; and I'll do it openly.

Enter SOLDIERS.

Bruce. Welcome all, heartily, most heartily.

Countess of Buchan (*to* 1*st Soldier*). Have you a wife?

1*st Soldier.* I have.

Countess of Buchan. You love her?

1*st Soldier.* Yes.

Countess of Buchan. Is not the truest love the most capricious?

1*st Soldier.* I cannot tell. True love is fanciful.

Countess of Buchan. You long to kiss your wife?

1*st Soldier.* And if I do,
What matters to your ladyship?

Countess of Buchan. (*whispering*). This, sir:
I also long to kiss one whom I love;
Perhaps I never shall; but I think now
In kissing you that I am kissing him.

> [*Kisses him.*

1st Soldier. Thanks, noble lady. If you were my wife
I'd kiss you thus.

> [*He embraces and kisses her.*

Bruce. Well said and bravely done!

Countess of Buchan. And can you fight
As deftly as you kiss?

Bruce. I warrant him! Enough.
Your song, my lady Douglas; sing it now;
A love-song, something homely if you can.

Douglas. Sing "If she love me," sweetheart

Lady Douglas. Shall I? Well.
But you should sing it rather.

Douglas. No; sing you.

SONG.

Love, though tempests be unruly,
    Blooms as when the weather's fair:
If she love me truly, truly,
    She will love me in despair.

Is there aught endures here longer?
    Can true love end ever wrongly?
Death will make her love grow stronger,
    If she love me strongly, strongly.

Can scorn conquer love? Can shame?
    Though the meanest tower above me,
She will share my evil fame,
    If she love me, if she love me.

Enter a FORESTER.

Forester. A thousand men are on you, fly!

[*going*

Bruce. Stand, there!
Hold him! What thousand men? who lead them? speak—

Put out the fire—stamp on it, some of you.

[*The fire is trampled out and the* FORESTER *seized.*

Forester.   I know not; but I saw them in the wood
Stealthily marching.

Bruce.   Are they near?

Forester.   An hour
By time, for they are stumbling out a way.
There's half a mile or so of wood between.
If I had been their guide they had been here.

Bruce.   You know the paths so thoroughly?

Forester.   Blindfold.

Bruce.   Could you lead safely to Kildrummie castle
A band of twenty?

Forester.   When? to-night?

Bruce.   Just now.

Forester.   I think I could.   But tell me, sir : they say
That you're the king.   Now are you ?

Bruce.   I am he.

Forester. (*awkwardly.*)   What must I do ?

Bruce.   Wait patiently.—Good friends,
We'll yet postpone farewell.   A little way
Together in the wood—

Edward Bruce.   But must we fly ?
Ten are a thousand in a coward's sight;
And they may be our friends.   Defence even here
Were not too rash against a hundred.   What !
Is not despair achievement's mother ?   Why !
The high, black night, a shout, a sudden charge,
And we dispel this sheep-heart's fearful dream.

Bruce.   Upon us march the earls of Fife and
      Buchan,
With many hundred men. They have hunted
      us
For days, and I have known.   My spies are
      caught
I fear, or they had not arrived so close
Without our knowledge. (*To Forester*). We
      must thank you, friend,
For timely intimation of our plight.
The plan I formed still holds, and this is it.
Kildrummie will give shelter to our wives ;
Nigel will take them there : Douglas, one
      way,
And I, another, as we may decide,
Splits up the scent,—and we shall all escape.

Edward Bruce.   Brother and king—

Bruce.   No more.   In straits like these
Counsel's a Syren : if the leader list,
Wreck follows.   Errant paths, straightly
      pursued,

Soon reach the goal; while wiser, well-thought
    ways
Wander about for fear of miry shoes.
And shall I hear one rasher than myself,
When wisdom would be folly!—Isabella,
A little way together, then farewell.—

                                [*To Forester.*

Friend, go before us.—Follow close. No
    word
Above a whisper.

Isabella. Must I leave you then?
Why are we made so that we trust our hopes!

                                        [*Exeunt.*

ACT V.

Scene I.—*A passage in* Berwick Castle. *Enter* Crombe *as jailor, carrying food. He opens a door, and the* Countess of Buchan *is discovered in a cage.*

Countess of Buchan. (*aside*). O me!
  Another! I can court no more.
This one I'll take by storm.—Fellow, good
  friend,
I think you are my thousandth jailor. Soon
I'll have a fresh one doubtless every day.
I've here had trial of my power on men,
On common vulgar men like you—for you
Are like your predecessors, I suppose—
And find myself most potent. Listen, now!
Yes, but you shall, you must; and look as
  well:
For I have looks like golden lightning, swift,

Gentle and perilous, that fascinate
The worshipful beholder.   I have words,
Sweet words, soft words, and words like two-
    edged swords,
Like singing winds that rock the sense asleep,
Like waves full-breasted, filling deepest souls ;
And I will kill you in a thousand ways
With words and looks unless you yield you
    now.
The others all were conquered just too late ;
The women tell me nothing—English all ;
But you will tell me what I want to know,
In brave submission to my witchery ;
Now, like a man : I hope you are a man.

Crombe.   What must I tell you ?

Countess of Buchan.   You must tell me first
How the king is—King Robert Bruce, I
    mean.

Crombe.   They say he's well.

Countess of Buchan.   Where is he then ?
    But sir,

I see you better now; you have an eye,
A brow, a mouth. Without more question, say
How Scotland fares since I was prisoned here.

Crombe. Because of this same eye, and brow, and mouth
They made me jailor.

Countess of Buchan. O, I understand !
And being nobler than those stolid pikes—
Pike-handles, I should say—forerunning you,
You'll not do wrong in duty's name. Escape
You cannot help me to; but tell me, sir,
Some news.

Crombe. Ah! Pardon me. If, as you say,
I have a brain to know that wrong is wrong
Though soldierly obedience be its badge,
Shall I not have the strength to overcome
Rebellious righteousness? Think you—

Countess of Buchan. James Crombe !

Crombe.   Your servant ever, lady.

Countess of Buchan.   Pardon, friend ;
I did not know you.   I've no memory
Except for horrors.   I am half a beast—
Starved, frozen, scorched, in rags. Sometimes at night
I'm mad.   The rotten air, the subtle dark,
The clammy cold, crawl through my blood like worms :
They knot themselves in aches, they gnaw my flesh,
And I believe me dead.   Ghosts visit me :
They come in undistinguishable throngs,
Sighing and moaning like a windy wood.
Demons invade my grave with flaming eyes,
With lolling tongues ; and ugly horrors steam
And whirl about me.   Mountains topple down,
Grazing my head ; and threatening worlds approach,
But never whelm me.   O my friend ! O me!
Tell me for mercy's sake of living men!
How came you here ?

Crombe. To be beside you, lady.

Countess of Buchan. What! You are weeping! Dear friend, speak to me.
What food is this? White bread, and wine, and meat!
(*Clapping her hands.*) Thanks, thanks! O thanks! I'll eat, while you recount
All, all, about my friends!

Crombe. My time is brief.
And first I'll tell you of an enemy.
Edward the First is dead.

Countess of Buchan. Say you! Aha!
That was a mighty villain.

Crombe. Nigel is dead.
They killed him when they took Kildrummie tower.

Countess of Buchan. Ah, what a wanton waste of noble blood!
Remorseless tigers! Ah, the wolves, the rats!—
The queen, and lady Douglas?

Crombe.   Prisoners both.

Countess of Buchan.   The man, my husband?

Crombe.   Beaten, decayed, forgot.
When we were scattered in the wood of
    Drome,
The king sought refuge in an Irish isle,
Which in the spring he left, and dared his fate.
So after perils, and trials, and mighty acts,
And deeds of marvellous device—well poised
By those achievements, rare and manifold,
Heroically wrought by Edward Bruce,
Douglas, Boyd, Fraser, Gilbert de la Haye,
Randolf, and many another famous knight,
Whose deeds already ring in lands afar—
At Inverury he and your husband met:
And there the earl suffered such dread defeat,
That ignominy has become the grave
Where all his hopes lie buried.

Countess of Buchan.   Wretched soul!

Crombe.   Now in the length and breadth of
    this free land,

One castle only is in England's power.
Would I had time to tell you how 'twas done!

Countess of Buchan. What castle?

Crombe. Stirling. Edward found the siege
For his hot blood too long, and made a pact,
That if the governor, Sir Philip Mowbray,
Were not relieved within a year and day,
He should surrender. In the interval
Sir Philip went to London to the king—
Edward the Second, an unstable man—
And couched his eyes of that security
That curtained Scotland's state. He levied soon
The mightiest army ever England raised;
And in the sight of Stirling Bruce and he
Are met to fight.

Countess of Buchan. Now?

Crombe. Now. And news is come
That Bruce to-day o'erthrew a champion
Between the armies; and that Randolf fought

And conquered Clifford, who had dreadful
    odds.

Countess of Buchan.   And are they fighting
    now?

Crombe.   No; but to-morrow
The battle is.

Countess of Buchan.   Then, gallant friend,
    away!
Take horse and ride!   You must not miss
    to-morrow.
Spur through the night!—Nay, think no more
    of me!
Or think me sitting lightsome on the croup,
And smiling at the moon.   I go with you:
My soul is in your arm—You must not stay.
One stout heart more!—Ride, ride!—I thank
    you, friend:
To know your dear and steadfast constancy,
As now I do, is worth these lonely years.—
Away to victory!—I can weep at last!—
Here, take this withered rag!   It is the scarf

The queen gave me that far-off night in
   Drome.
My parched and desert ēyes that sorrow shrunk
Are wet with happiness! See! Am I red?
My pale and stagnant blood wakes up again,
I would that we were flying together, Crombe,
As once we did, rebels, so free and glad!
Now go! Now go!—Yes, kiss me through
   the bars.
My kiss shall help to win the battle. Go!

> [*He kisses her, and exit. The
>   scene closes.*

Scene II.—*The* Scottish Camp *at Bannock-
burn.* Bruce *in his tent at night.*

Bruce. This drowned and abject mood; this
   sodden brain;
This broken-back; this dull insanity,
That mopes and broods and has no thought
   at all;

This dross, that, in exchange for molten gold
Of madness thrice refined, were hell for
    heaven ;
This flabby babe; this hare; this living
    death ;
This sooty-hued, cold-blooded melancholy !
We know it for a subtle, potent lie—
A vapour, a mere mood ! But when it comes,
Stealing upon us like unwelcome sleep
In high festivity, we've no more power
To shake our souls alive, than if we'd drunk
Of Lapland philtres,—muddy brew of hell !
When we, like beakers brimmed with wine,
    are full
Of living in the hand of fate, there strikes
An image through the brain that destines us,
And in the careless instant we are spilled
To be replenished never : so we feel.
We feel ? How hard it is to fix the mind !
Only less hard than to withdraw it. Sleep ?
No; not to-night. Heart, faithless heart,
    grow strong.
Ay, now I have remembrance of a thought

A dear breath whispered making wisdom
   sweet.
How did she say it? "Darling" was it?
   No.
"Sweetheart," or "dear," or "dearest?"
   Which of all
Those thin worn words that love assays, and
   coins
Anew, began her little earnest speech?
Ah, it was that name, fond and passionate,
Tender and confident, poor milkmaids use,
And dream not that a queen can find no
   sweeter.
"Dearie," she said, "when faith is strong in
   you,
Then only have you any right to think,
To judge, to act." And kissed me then, as
   if
Her healing truth had need of honey! O,
Love with its simple glance can pierce the
   night,
When drowsy sages at their tapers nod!
I will not trust myself but when self-trust
Is buoyant in me. And I surely know

To-morrow's battle finds one soul sufficient.—
I wonder how my wife is ! Have these years,
These days, these hours—it is the hours that
    tell—
Dealt kindly with her in her nunnery?
Poor lady ! She is gentle, delicate—
A lute that can respond to nothing harsh.
If she be shattered by this heavy stroke
Of separation ! I, with sinewy strings,
Endure the constant quivering—

       (*Enter Guard*).
                  What now?

Guard. The leaders wait without, your
    majesty.

Bruce. Is it that time? Well, bid them
    enter.

[*Enter* EDWARD BRUCE, DOUGLAS, RANDOLF,
    and WALTER THE STEWARD.

                    Friends,
Good morning. Let me see your eyes.—
    Randolf

You have not slept.—Sir James, perhaps you
   have :
Your eyes were never dull.—What, half
   awake !
Why, Walter, love, if not anxiety,
Should have kept watch in that young head
   of yours !
Brother, I know you slept.

Edward Bruce. Why should I not ?
I thanked God for the error that I made
In giving respite to the garrison,
Since it has brought us to this desperate pass
Where we must conquer. Then I slept, and
   dreamt ;
And wakened, laughing at I know not what.

Randolf. I had no sleep. This would not
   leave my mind,
That we were one to five.

Bruce. Why Randolf, shame !
You are the last who should complain of that.
What good knight was it, like a water-drop,

Lost shape and being in an English sea,
Which found him out a rock, but yesterday?
Why man, you are my cousin, Thomas
    Randolf;
And this is Douglas; this, my brother
    Edward;
We are men who have done deeds, God
    helping us.
God helping us, we'll do a deed to-day!

Randolf. I do not fear; but lonely, in the
    night
I could not see how we must win.

Bruce. No! come.

    [*They go to the door of the tent and
        look out.*

I see the battle as it will be fought.
The sun climbs up behind us. If he shine,
His beams will strike on English eyes. Look
    there!
The earth throws off her mourning nightly
    weed;

And the fresh dawn, her bowermaid, coyly
    comes
To veil her with the morning, like a bride
Worthy the sun's embrace. This fight you
    dread,
Regard it as a happy tournament
Played at the marriage of the fragrant world,
If the full weight and awe of its intent
Press on you too o'erwhelmingly.

Randolf. Not I.
I'd rather lose the fight for what it is,
Than win it jestingly.

Bruce. Well said! The night,
That filled you with its gloom, out of your
    blood
Exhales, and it is day. Imagine, now:
Between high Stirling and the Bannock
    stream,
Whose silvery streak hot blood will tarnish
    soon,
Four battles stand. To westward, Edward's
    charge,

Douglas and Walter to the north and east,
Randolf, the doubter, in the central van ;
I keep the second ward. Pent in this space
We cannot be outflanked, the river's gorge
On this wing, and on that, calthrops and pits.
The English archers scattered—Edward's task—
There but remains to stand, while yonder host,
Which leaves its revel only now, shall twine,
And knot, entangled in its proper coils,
Crammed in a cage too small for such a bulk,
Such sinuous length, such strength, to bustle in,
Save to its own confusion and dismay.
Speak I not reasonably, and quietly ?

Randolf. Too quietly for me ! Why, in this trap,
This coffin, they shall die for want of air !

Edward Bruce. It is too cheap a victory !

Douglas. When won,
I hope we may not find it all too dear.

[*Bagpipes, drums, trumpets.*

Bruce.   Ha! now the din begins!   My blood
   is lit!
Come, let us set our soldiers in a glow!
After the abbot says the battle mass,
I'll speak to them, and touch them with a
   flame.

Douglas.   They'll burn.

Edward Bruce.   They'll make a bon-fire.

Walter the Steward.   To announce
That Scotland's liberty's of age.

Bruce.   Well roared,
My lioncel!

[*Exeunt.*

Scene III.—*The* Field of Bannockburn.
   Enter Edward II., the Earl of
   Pembroke, Sir Giles De Argentine,

> SIR INGRAM DE UMFRAVILLE, *with other lords and knights, in advance of the English lines.*

Edward II. Will yon men fight?

Umfraville. Ay, siccarly. My liege,
If you will hear an old man's humble word
Who knows the Scotchmen well, feign a retreat:
Then will these fiery children of the north—
Children they are in every gift save strength,
And most in guileless daring—rush on us,
Leaving their vantage, and be overcome
Utterly, as in many a fight before.

Edward II. I'm a young warrior, and I mean to win
By dint of strength, and not by strategy.
To sneak a victory I came not north;
But in a lordly way to overthrow
The base usurper of my lordship here.
Leave paltry sleights and fawnings upon chance

To starveling rebels, keen as hungry curs
That dodge the whip, and steal the bone at
    once.
Think you we brought our friends across the
    sea
To juggle with them? We are here to fight,
As in the lists, like gentlemen. My lords,
I give you Scotland. Nothing for myself
Save sovereignty I claim; and that must be
Not snared by ambush, for assassins fit,
But seized by courage, frank and English.

Pembroke. Sire,
One reason only urges strategy:
Adopting it, less English blood will flow.

Edward II. That touches me.

De Argentine. And it is kindly thought.
But I have heard the Scotsmen plume them-
    selves
On victory over any English odds,
In battles, pitched, embroiled, and hand to
    hand;

That we have never vanquished them in fight
Except when treachery assisted arms.
Conquest unchallengeable, dearly bought
Were worth its cost. A wily victory
Would leave our foes unhumbled, unappeased,
And confident of ultimate success.

Edward II. This is the wisest counsel.

Umfraville. Hear me yet.
What warrior is wilier than Bruce?
The schiltron he has perfected. No knights
Can break the Scottish spearmen. Chivalry
Means nought for them save mounted foes whose trust
Is in their horses—

Edward II. 'Tis a base device,
This slaughter of our steeds! A dastard's trick!
The delicate art of war, where excellence
Lay in the power of noble blood alone,
He makes a trade for ploughmen. Battle-fields

Are shambles since this rebel taught his clowns
To fear not knighthood!

Umfraville. True indeed, my liege!
And some have thought that this new style of
 war
Will drive the other out. But see you not
That every possible advantage—

Edward II. No!
For I will not!—Behold, the Scots ask mercy!

Umfraville. They do—from heaven. These
 men will win or die.

Edward II. I hate such kneeling, whining
 warriors, I!
What right have they to think God on their
 side?
Our glorious father taught them otherwise
With iteration one had deemed enough.
I burn to teach them finally. My lords,
Our swords shall pray for us. One hour's
 hot work,

And Scotland is your own. Let us begin!
Each to his post, and everlasting shame
Blight him who cherishes a moment's thought
Of other means of victory than these,
Our English bows and lances, English hearts,
And not less English courage of our friends
Whose foreign banners grace our army.
  Come;
England shall stretch from Orkney to Land's End
After to-day. St. George for Merry England!

[*Exeunt.*

SCENE IV.—*Another part of the* FIELD. *The Scottish army. Enter* BRUCE *and the other leaders.*

Bruce.   I think we all know well what courage is:
Not thews, not blood, not bulk, not bravery:
Its highest title, patience. Fiery haste

Has lost most battles. Till the word be given,
Let no man charge to-day. No seeming flight
Must lead you to pursue. Take root; grow
    strong;
The earth is Scottish. For our country stand
Like bastioned, frowning rocks that beard the
    sea,
And triumph everlastingly. Doubt not
The time to charge will come—once and
    straight home:
We'll need no spur: so must you curb your
    blood;
Command your anguished strength: a false
    start now
Will lose a race we cannot run again.
If any of you feel unfit for fight
From any cause whatever, let him go,
Leaving us undiluted. Scorn nor curse
Shall blast him; but our generous thought
    shall praise
His act and consecrate his name,
As one who did his best in doing nought;
For victory depends on each of us.
I say, if gallant souls be timorous,

Get them behind the hill, and be not sad:
Great courage goes to make an open coward.

(*A great shout*).

Then are we all one heart.   Our enemies,
Our English enemies who hope to drown
The very name of Scot in Scottish blood,
And those outlandish battle-harlots, hired
From Holland, Zealand, Brabant, Normandy,
Those Picards, Flemings, Gascons, Guiennese,
The refuse of the realms from which they
　　swarm,
Are robbers lured by plunder, one and all,
From king to scullion: they are in the
　　wrong.
We are the weapon to defend the right
God grasps to-day.   Can we be put to shame?

Soldiers.   No!

Bruce.   Forward, trusty friends!   The hour
　　is come
For long-desired redemption of the vows
Groaned out when tender mothers, sisters,
　　wives,

Fathers we worshipped, brothers we adored,
Were spared not.   Let our battle-cry be—
  no ;
I'll give you none.   Each soldier shout the
  name.
Of that best friend in prison buried quick ;
Of yonder heaven-homed, most beloved soul
Among the multitude whose butchered limbs
Lie pledged in sepulchres.   My countrymen,
Welcome to victory, which must be ours,
For death is freedom !

Soldiers.   Victory or death !
          [Exeunt.

SCENE V.—*The* GILLIES' HILL.   *Men and women watching the battle.*

A Young Friar.   "St. Andrew and St.
  George !   Fight on !   fight on !"
A whole year's storms let loose on one small
  lake

Prisoned among the mountains, rioting
Between the heathery slopes and rugged cliffs,
Dragging the water from its deepest lair,
Shaking it out like feathers on the blast;
With shock on shock of thunder; shower on shower
Of jagged and sultry lightning; banners, crests,
Of rainbows torn and streaming, tossed and flung
From panting surge to surge; where one strong sound,
Enduring with continuous piercing shriek
Whose pitch is ever heightened, still escapes
Wroth from the roaring whirl of elements;
Where mass and motion, flash and colour spin,
Wrapped and confounded in their blent array:
And this all raving on a summer morn,
With unseen larks beside the golden sun,
And merest blue above; with not a breeze
To fan the burdened rose-trees, or incense
With mimic rage the foamless rivulet,

That like a little child goes whispering
Along the woodland ways its happy thought ;
Were no more wild, grotesque, fantastical,
Uncouth, unnatural—and I would think
Impossible, but for the vision here—
Than is this clamorous and unsightly war,
Where swords and lances, shields and arrows, flash,
Whistle, and clang—splintered like icicles,
Eclipsed like moons, broken like reeds, like flames—
Lewd flames that lick themselves in burning lust—
With scorpion tongues lapping the lives of men ;
Where axes cut to hearts worth all the oaks ;
Where steel burns blue, and golden armours blaze—
One moment so, the next, a ruddier hue ;
Where broidered banners rustle in the charge,
And deck the carnage out——A skeleton,
Ribboned and garlanded may sweetly suit
The morris-dancers for a May-pole now !—
Where hoofs of horses spatter brains of men,

And beat dull thunder from the shaking sod;
Where yelling pibrochs, braying trumpets,
    drums,
And shouts, and shrieks, and groans, hoarse,
    shrill—a roar
That shatters hearing—echo to the sky;
Where myriad ruthless vessels, freighted full
Of proud rich blood—with images of God,
Their reasoning souls, deposed from their
    command—
By winds of cruel hate usurped and urged,
Are driven upon each other, split, and
    wrecked,
And foundered deep as hell. The air is dark
With souls. I cannot look—I cannot see.

         [*Kneels.*

A Woman. The battle's lost before it's well
    begun.
Our men fall down in ranks like barley-rigs
Before a dense wet blast.

A Cripple. Despair itself
Can only die before the English bows.

O that they could come at them! Who are
    these
That skirt the marsh?

Woman. My sight is weak. But see;
Here's an old fellow, trembling, muttering. Look.
How he is strung; and what an eye he has!

Cripple. Old sight sees well away. I warrant,
    now,
His is a perfect mirror of the fight.
You see well, father?

Old Man. Ay. That's Edward Bruce;
And none too soon. The feathered deaths
    speed thick
In jubilant choirs, flight after singing flight.
That tune must end; the nest be harried.
    Ride,
Fiery Edward! Yet our staunch hearts quail
    not.
Ah! now the daze begins! I know it well.
The cloth-yard shafts like magic shuttles,
    weave

Athwart the warped air dazzling, dire dismay,
And the beholder's blood slinks to his heart
Like moles from daylight; all his sinews fade
To unsubstantial tinder. Ha! spur! spur!
There are ten thousand bowmen! Gallop!
    Charge!
Now, by the soul of Wallace, Edward Bruce,
    The battle's balanced! On your sword it
        hangs!
Look you; there's fighting! Just a minute's
        fight!
Tug, strain! Throe after throe! Travail of
        war!
The birth—defeat and victory, those twins,
That in an instant breathe and die, and leave
So glorious and so dread a memory!—
The bowstring's cut! What butchery to see!
They shear them down these English yeomen!
    God!
It looks like child's play too! And so it feels,
Now I remember me.—That's victory.
An English army is a mighty bow;
The bowmen are the string; the string is cut;
The weapon's useless!

Woman. But the knights, the knights!

Old Man. I see them. But our spearmen!
    Do you see!
This hill we stand on trembles with the shock:
They budge not, planted, founded in the soil.
Another charge! Now watch! Now see!
    Ugh! Ha!
Did one spear flicker? One limb waver?
    No!
These fellows there are fighting for their land!
The English army through its cumbrous bulk
Thrilled and astounded to the utmost rear,
Twists like a snake, and folds into itself,
Rank pushed through rank. Now are they
    hand to hand!
How short a front! How close! They're
    sewn together
With steel cross-stitches, halbert over sword,
Spear across lance, and death the purfled
    seam!
I never saw so fierce, so locked a fight!
That tireless brand that like a pliant flail

Threshes the lives from sheaves of English-
    men,
Know you who wields it? Douglas, who
    but he!
A noble meets him now. Clifford it is!
No bitterer foes seek out each other there.
Parried! That told! and that! Clifford,
    good night!
And Douglas shouts to Randolf; Edward
    Bruce
Cheers on the Steward; while the king's
    voice rings
In every Scotch ear: such a narrow strait
Confines this firth of war!

Young Friar. God gives me strength
Again to gaze with eyes unseared. Jewels!
These must be jewels peering in the grass,
Cloven from helms, or on them: dead men's
    eyes
Scarce shine so bright. The banners dip and
    mount
Like masts at sea. The battle-field is slime,
A ruddy lather beaten up with blood!

Men slip; and horses, stuck with shafts like butts,
Sprawl, madly shrieking! No, I cannot look!
> [*Exit.*

Woman. Look here! look here, I say!
Who's this behind?
His horse sinks down—the brute is dead, I think.
His clothes are torn; his face with dust and sweat
Encrusted, baked, and cracked. He speaks; he shouts;
And shouting runs this way. He's mad, I think.

Cripple. He's made his hearers mad. Tents, blankets, poles,
Pitch-forks, and staves, and knives, brandished and spread
By women, children, grandsires! What is this?

> *Enter* CROMBE *followed by a crowd bearing blankets for banners, and armed with staves, etc.*

Crombe. I rode all night to strike a blow to-
    day:
The noblest lady living bade me go:
Her kiss is on my lips and in my soul.
Come after me—yea, with your naked hands,
And conquer weapons!
                  [*Exeunt, shouting.*

SCENE VI.—*The* FIELD OF BANNOCKBURN.
    The Scotch Reserve. To them enter
    BRUCE.

Bruce. Most noble souls who wait so
    patiently!
Your splendid faith is in the air about you;
Your steady eyes shine like a galaxy;
Your presence comforts me: pressed in the
    fight,
The thought of you, like balm upon a wound,
Softened the thriftless aching of my heart.
The English waver; on the hill behind
Our followers fright them, marching in array,
Bannered and armed, a legion out of heaven.

The tide of battle turns, and victory
Needs only you to launch it bravely forth.
Now—I would bid you think, but that the
   thought
Eludes me, like a homely, old-known song,
Wreathing in fitful gusts beyond the sense—
Now will the lofty keystone of our life
Be pitched in heaven for ever. We have
   dreamt
Our prayers into fulfilment many a time:
To-day we wrestle, and the victory's ours:
And yet I feel so scantly what it means,
That I'm ashamed. Enough: I know you
   all.—
Now for our homes, our children, and our
   wives,
For freedom, for our land, for victory!
And cry our old cry, Carrick!

Soldiers.   Carrick and victory!
                              [*Exeunt.*

THE END.

By the same Author.

Crown 8vo. Sewed. Price One Shilling.

THE NORTH WALL
By JOHN DAVIDSON.

EXTRACTS FROM SOME LITERARY NOTICES.

"This is a most absorbing tale. It is fresh, manly, robust. Its perusal is a tonic, a stimulus, an inspiration. It is just the thing for the tourist and the traveller. It is vivacious, original, wholesome. It deserves to be placed side by side with 'Called Back.' It is sure to become very popular."—*Oldham Chronicle.*

"This is the maddest tale we have read for an age."—*Literary World.*

"As a first book it is full of promise. The plot is wild enough in all conscience; wild to the verge of burlesque; but it is, it must be allowed, thoroughly original, and in the working of it out we have both wit and humour displayed. The writer will do better things yet; he shows himself possessed of the stuff out of which good novelists are made. Time will develop his capabilities, and teach him self-restraint. In 'The North Wall' he is quite prodigal of his strength. Interspersed through the narrative, but not too obtrusively, are several touches of description of scenery and scenic effects that are very neatly put in."—*Glasgow Herald.*

"The humour and racy character of the writing are in the best tone. 'Miss Jane' is splendid. For railway journey or hour of leisure, no better story will be found on the book-stall. A dramatised version of 'The North Wall' should be highly popular on the stage.'—*Perth Constitutional.*

"There is no doubt about the originality of the crazy plot. The hero is a novelist who rushes into crime in order to 'cause a novel to take place in the world.'"—*North British Daily Mail.*

"To begin with, when we say that Wilson & McCormick publish the book, we do the same thing as saying that it is neat, elegant, and as æsthetic as it can be made for the money. , . . We are able to say with a safe conscience that 'The North Wall' is an excellent book—well written, well published, and certain to be well read."—*Greenock Herald.*

"Mr. Lee (the unsuccessful author) sets to work to compose a novel in action, and commences with personating a rich man whom a street accident has placed at his discretion. A strong likeness between the two gives rise to the design, which leads to many bewildering *qui pro quos*, and much extravagantly comic business."—*Westminster Review.*

GLASGOW: WILSON & McCORMICK, SAINT VINCENT STREET.

List of Books
IN
Belles Lettres

1893

"A word must be said for the manner in which the publishers have produced the volume (*i.e.*, 'The Earth Fiend'), a sumptuous folio, printed by CONSTABLE, the etchings on Japanese paper by MR. GOULDING. The volume should add not only to MR. STRANG's fame but to that of MESSRS. ELKIN MATHEWS AND JOHN LANE, who are rapidly gaining distinction for their beautiful editions of belles-lettres."
Daily Chronicle, Sept. 24, 1892.

Referring to Mr. LE GALLIENNE's "English Poems" and "Silhouettes" by MR. ARTHUR SYMONS—"we only refer to them now to note a fact which they illustrate, and, which we have been observing of late, namely, the recovery to a certain extent of good taste in the matter of printing and binding books. These two books, which are turned out by MESSRS. ELKIN MATHEWS AND JOHN LANE, are models of artistic publishing, and yet they are simplicity itself. The books with their excellent printing and their very simplicity, make a harmony which is satisfying to the artistic sense."—*Sunday Sun*, Oct. 2, 1892.

"MR. LE GALLIENNE is a fortunate young gentleman. I don't know by what legerdemain he and his publishers work, but here, in an age as stony to poetry as the ages of Chatterton and Richard Savage, we find the full edition of his book sold before publication. How is it done, MESSRS. ELKIN MATHEWS AND JOHN LANE? for, without depreciating MR. LE GALLIENNE's sweetness and charm, I doubt that the marvel would have been wrought under another publisher. These publishers, indeed, produce books so delightfully that it must give an added pleasure to the hoarding of first editions."
KATHARINE TYNAN in the *Irish Daily Independent*.

"To MESSRS. ELKIN MATHEWS AND JOHN LANE almost more than to any other, we take it, are the thanks of the grateful singer especially due; for it is they who have managed, by means of limited editions and charming workmanship to impress book-buyers with the belief that a volume may have an æsthetic and commercial value. They have made it possible to speculate in the latest discovered poet as in a new company—with the difference that an operation in the former can be done with three half-crowns."
St. James's Gazette.

June 1893.

List of Books
IN
BELLES LETTRES
(Including some Transfers)

PUBLISHED BY

Elkin Mathews & John Lane

The Bodley Head

Vigo Street, London, W.

N.B.—The Authors and Publishers reserve the right of reprinting any book in this list if a second edition is called for, except in cases where a stipulation has been made to the contrary, and of printing a separate edition of any of the books for America irrespective of the numbers to which the English editions are limited.

ADDLESHAW (PERCY).
   POEMS. 12mo. 5s. net.   - [*In preparation.*

ANTÆUS.
   THE BACKSLIDER AND OTHER POEMS.   100 only, sm. 4to.
   7s. 6d. net.   [*Very few remain.*

BEECHING (H. C.), J. W. MACKAIL, &
   J. B. B. NICHOLS.
   LOVE IN IDLENESS, with Vignette by W. B. SCOTT. Fcap. 8vo, half vellum. 12s. net.   [*Very few remain.*
   Transferred by the Authors to the present Publishers.

BENSON (ARTHUR CHRISTOPHER).
POEMS. 500 copies, 12mo. 5s. net. [*In preparation.*

BENSON (EUGENE).
FROM THE ASOLAN HILLS. A Poem. 300 copies, imp. 16mo. 5s. net. [*Very few remain.*

BINYON (LAWRENCE).
POEMS. 12mo. 5s. net. [*In preparation.*

BOURDILLON (F. W.).
A LOST GOD. A Poem, with Illustrations by H. J. FORD. 500 copies, 8vo. 6s. net. [*Very few remain.*

BOURDILLON (F. W.).
AILES D'ALOUETTE. Poems printed at the private press of Rev. H. DANIEL, Oxford. 100 only, 16mo. £1 10s. net. [*Very few remain.*

BRIDGES (ROBERT).
THE GROWTH OF LOVE. Printed in Fell's old English type at the private press of Rev. H. DANIEL, Oxford. 100 only, fcap 4to. £2 12s. 6d. net. [*Very few remain.*

COLERIDGE (HON. STEPHEN).
THE SANCTITY OF CONFESSION. A Romance. 2nd edition, cr. 8vo. 3s. net. [*A few remain.*

CRANE (WALTER).
RENASCENCE: a Book of Verse. Frontispiece and 38 designs by the Author, imp. 16mo. 7s. 6d. net. [*Very few remain.* Also a few fcap. 4to. £1 1s. net. And a few fcap. 4to, Japanese vellum, £1 15s. net.

CROSSING (WM.).

THE ANCIENT CROSSES OF DARTMOOR. With 11 plates, 8vo, cloth. 4s. 6d. net. [*Very few remain.*

DAVIDSON (JOHN).

PLAYS: Scaramouch in Naxos: An Unhistorical Pastoral; A Romantic Farce. Post 8vo. 5s. net. [*A few remain.*
Transferred by the Author to the present Publishers.

DAVIDSON (JOHN).

FLEET ST. ECLOGUES. 2nd edition, fcap. 8vo, buckram. 5s. net.

DAVIDSON (JOHN).

BRUCE: A DRAMA IN FIVE ACTS. Fcap. 8vo. 5s. net.
The few remaining copies transferred by the Author to the present Publishers.

DAVIDSON (JOHN).

THE NORTH WALL. Fcap. 8vo. 2s. 6d. net.
The few remaining copies transferred by the Author to the present Publishers.

DE GRUCHY (AUGUSTA).

UNDER THE HAWTHORN AND OTHER VERSES. *Frontispiece by Walter Crane.* 300 copies, cr. 8vo. 5s. net. Also 30 copies on Japanese vellum. 15s. net.

DE TABLEY (LORD).

POEMS, DRAMATIC AND LYRICAL. By JOHN LEICESTER WARREN (Lord De Tabley), illustrations and cover design by C. S. RICKETTS. 2nd edition, cr. 8vo. 7s. 6d. net.

DIAL (THE).

No. 1 of the second series. Illustrations by RICKETTS, SHANNON, PISSARRO, 200 only, 4to. £1 1s. net.
[*Very few remain.*

The present series will be continued at irregular intervals.

FIELD (MICHAEL).

SIGHT AND SONG (Poems on Pictures). 400 copies 12mo. 5s. net.
[*Very few remain.*

FIELD (MICHAEL).

STEPHANIA: A TRIALOGUE IN 3 ACTS. 250 copies pott 4to. 6s. net.
[*Very few remain.*

GALE (NORMAN).

ORCHARD SONGS. Fcap. 8vo, with title-page and cover design by WILL ROTHENSTEIN. 5s. net.
Also a special edition limited in number on small paper (Whatman) bound in English vellum. £1 1s. net.
[*In preparation.*

GOSSE (EDMUND).

THE LETTERS OF THOMAS LOVELL BEDDOES. Now first edited, cr. 8vo.
[*In preparation.*

GRAHAME (KENNETH).

PAGAN PAPERS: A VOLUME OF ESSAYS. Cr. 8vo. 5s. net.
[*In preparation.*

GREENE (G. A.).

ITALIAN LYRISTS OF TO-DAY. Translations in the original metres from about 35 living Italian poets with bibliographical and biographical notes, cr. 8vo. 5s. net.
[*In preparation.*

HAKE (T. GORDON).

A Selection from his Poems. Edited by Mrs. Meynell, cr. 8vo. 5s. net. [*In preparation.*

HALLAM (ARTHUR HENRY).

The Poems, together with his essay "On Some of the Characteristics of Modern Poetry and on the Lyrical Poems of Alfred Tennyson." Edited, with an introduction, by Richard Le Gallienne. 550 copies, fcap. 8vo. 5s. net. [*Very few remain.*

HAMILTON (COL. IAN).

The Ballad of Hadji and Other Poems. Etched frontispiece by Wm. Strang. 550 copies, 12mo. 3s. net. *Transferred by the Author to the present Publishers.*

HAYES (ALFRED).

The Vale of Arden and Other Poems. Fcap. 8vo. 5s. net. [*In preparation*

HICKEY (EMILY H.).

Verse Tales, Lyrics and Translations. 300 pages, imp. 16mo. 5s. net.

HORNE (HERBERT P.).

Diversi Colores. Poems, with ornaments by the Author, 250 copies, 16mo. 5s. net.

IMAGE (SELWYN).

Carols and Poems, with decorations by H. P. Horne. 250 copies. 5s. net. [*In preparation.*

JOHNSON (EFFIE).

In the Fire and Other Fancies. Frontispiece by Walter Crane. 500 copies, imp. 16mo. 3s. 6d. net.

JOHNSON (LIONEL).

THE ART OF THOMAS HARDY. Six Essays, with etched portrait by WM. STRANG, and Bibliography by JOHN LANE, cr. 8vo. 5s. 6d. net.
Also 150 copies, large paper, with proofs of the portrait £1. 1s. net. [Very shortly.

JOHNSON (LIONEL).

A VOLUME OF POEMS. 12mo. 5s. net. [In preparation.

KEATS (JOHN).

THREE ESSAYS, now issued in book form for the first time. Edited by H. BUXTON FORMAN, with life-mask by HAYDON. Fcap 4to. 10s. 6d. net. [Very few remain.

LEATHER (R. K.).

VERSES. 250 copies fcap. 8vo. 3s. net.

Transferred by the Author to the present Publishers.

LEATHER (R. K.), & RICHARD LE GALLIENNE.

THE STUDENT AND THE BODY-SNATCHER AND OTHER TRIFLES. 250 copies, roy. 18mo. 3s. net.
Also 50 copies, large paper, 7s. 6d. net. [Very few remain.

LE GALLIENNE (RICHARD).

PROSE FANCIES. With cover design and title-page by WILL ROTHENSTEIN. 5s. net. Also a limited large paper edition. 12s. 6d. net. [In preparation.

LE GALLIENNE (RICHARD).

THE BOOK BILLS OF NARCISSUS. An account rendered by RICHARD LE GALLIENNE. 2nd edition, cr. 8vo, buckram. 5s.

LE GALLIENNE (RICHARD).

English Poems. 2nd edition, 12mo. 5s. net.

LE GALLIENNE (RICHARD).

George Meredith: some Characteristics; with a Bibliography (much enlarged) by John Lane, portrait, &c. 3rd edition, cr. 8vo. 5s. 6d. net.

LE GALLIENNE (RICHARD).

The Religion of a Literary Man. Fcap. 8vo. 3s. 6d. Also a special edition on hand-made paper. 10s. 6d. net.
[*In preparation.*

LETTERS TO LIVING ARTISTS.

500 copies, fcap. 8vo. 3s. 6d. net. [*Very few remain.*

MARSTON (PHILIP BOURKE).

A Last Harvest: Lyrics and Sonnets from the Book of Life Edited by Louise Chandler Moulton. 500 copies, post 8vo. 5s. net.
Also 50 copies on large paper, hand-made. 10s. 6d. net.
[*Very few remain.*

MARTIN (W. WILSEY).

Quatrains, Life's Mystery and Other Poems. 16mo. 2s. 6d. net. [*Very few remain.*

MARZIALS (THEO.).

The Gallery of Pigeons and Other Poems. Post 8vo. 4s. 6d. net. [*Very few remain.*
Transferred by the Author to the present Publishers.

MEYNELL (MRS.), (ALICE C. THOMPSON).

Poems. 2nd edition, fcap. 8vo. 3s. 6d. net. A few of the 50 large paper copies (1st edition) remain. 12s. 6d. net.

MEYNELL (MRS.).

THE RHYTHM OF LIFE AND OTHER ESSAYS. 2nd edition, fcap. 8vo. 3s. 6d. *net.* A few of the 50 large paper copies (1st edition) remain, 12s. 6d. *net.*

MURRAY (ALMA).

PORTRAIT AS BEATRICE CENCI. With critical notice containing four letters from ROBERT BROWNING. 8vo, wrapper. 2s. *net.*

NETTLESHIP (J. T.).

ROBERT BROWNING. Essays and Thoughts. Third edition, cr. 8vo. 5s. 6d. *net.* Half a dozen of the Whatman L.P. copies (first edition) remain, £1 1s. *net.* .

NOBLE (JAS. ASHCROFT).

THE SONNET IN ENGLAND AND OTHER ESSAYS. Title-page and cover design by AUSTIN YOUNG. 600 copies, cr. 8vo. 5s. *net.* Also 50 copies L.P. 12s. 6d. *net.*

NOEL (HON. RODEN).

POOR PEOPLE'S CHRISTMAS. 250 copies. 16mo. 1s. *net.*
[*Very few remain.*

OXFORD CHARACTERS.

A series of lithographed portraits by WILL ROTHENSTEIN, with text by F. YORK POWELL and others. To be issued monthly in term. Each number will contain two portraits. Part I. ready June 1893, will contain portraits of SIR HENRY ACLAND, K.C.B, F.R.S., M.D., and of Mr. W. A. L. FLETCHER, of Christ Church, Captain of the University Boat Club. 350 copies only, folio, wrapper, 5s. *net* per part; 50 special copies containing proof impressions of the portraits signed by the artist, 10s. 6d. *net* per part.

PINKERTON (PERCY).

GALEAZZO: A Venetian Episode and other Poems. Etched frontispiece. 16mo. 5s. *net.* [*Very few remain.*
Transferred by the Author to the present Publishers.

RADFORD (DOLLIE).
    SONGS. A new volume of verse.   [*In preparation*.

RADFORD (ERNEST).
    CHAMBERS TWAIN. Frontispiece by WALTER CRANE. 250 copies. Imp. 16mo. 5s. *net.*
    Also 50 copies large paper, 10s. 6d. *net.*   [*Very few remain.*

RHYMERS' CLUB, THE BOOK OF THE.
    A second series is in preparation.

SCHAFF (DR. P.).
    LITERATURE AND POETRY: Papers on Dante, etc. Portrait and Plates, 100 copies only. 8vo. 10s. *net.*

SCOTT (WM. BELL).
    A POET'S HARVEST HOME: WITH AN AFTERMATH. 300 copies, 12mo. 5s. *net.*   [*Very few remain.*
    * *Will not be reprinted.*

STODDARD (R. H.).
    THE LION'S CUB; WITH OTHER VERSE. Portrait. 100 copies only, bound in an illuminated Persian design. Fcap. 8vo. 5s. *net.*   [*Very few remain.*

SYMONDS (JOHN ADDINGTON).
    IN THE KEY OF BLUE, AND OTHER PROSE ESSAYS. Cover design by C. S. RICKETTS. 2nd edition, thick cr. 8vo. 8s. 6d. *net.*

THOMPSON (FRANCIS).
    A VOLUME OF POEMS. 12mo. 5s. *net.*   [*In preparation.*

TODHUNTER (JOHN).
    A SICILIAN IDYLL. Frontispiece by WALTER CRANE. 250 copies. Imp. 16mo. 5s. *net.*
    Also 50 copies large paper, fcap. 4to. 10s. 6d. *net.*
                            [*Very few remain.*

TOMSON (GRAHAM R.).

AFTER SUNSET. A volume of Poems. 12mo. 5s. net.
Also a limited large paper edition. 12s. 6d. net.
[In preparation.

TREE (H. BEERBOHM).

THE IMAGINATIVE FACULTY, a Lecture delivered at the Royal Institution. With portrait of Mr. TREE from an unpublished drawing by the Marchioness of Granby. Fcap. 8vo, boards. 2s. 6d. net. *[Immediately.*

TYNAN (KATHARINE).

A NEW VOLUME OF POEMS. 5s. net. *[In preparation.*

VAN DYKE (HENRY).

THE POETRY OF TENNYSON. 3rd edition, enlarged, cr. 8vo. 5s. 6d. net.

The late Laureate himself gave valuable aid in correcting various details.

WATSON (WILLIAM).

THE ELOPING ANGELS: A CAPRICE. Second edition, sq. 16mo, buckram. 3s. 6d. net.

WATSON (WILLIAM).

EXCURSIONS IN CRITICISM; BEING SOME PROSE RECREATIONS OF A RHYMER. 2nd edition, 12mo. 5s. net.

WATSON (WILLIAM).

THE PRINCE'S QUEST, AND OTHER POEMS. With a bibliographical note added. 2nd edition, 12mo. 4s. 6d. net.

WEDMORE (FREDERICK).

PASTORALS OF FRANCE — RENUNCIATIONS. A volume of Stories. Title-page by JOHN FULLEYLOVE, R.I. Cr. 8vo. 5s. net. *[In preparation.*

A few of the large paper copies of Renunciations (1st edition) remain, 10s. 6d. net.

WICKSTEED (P. H.).

    DANTE: SIX SERMONS. 3rd edition cr. 8vo. 2s. net.

WILDE (OSCAR).

    THE SPHINX. A Poem decorated throughout in line and colour and bound in a design by CHARLES RICKETTS. 250 copies £2 2s. net. 25 copies large paper, £5. 5s. net.
    [*In preparation.*

WILDE (OSCAR).

    The incomparable and ingenious history of Mr. W. H., being the true secret of Shakespear's sonnets now for the first time here fully set forth, with initial letters and cover design by CHARLES RICKETTS. 500 copies 10s. 6d. net. Also 50 copies large paper, 21s. net. [*In preparation.*

WILDE (OSCAR).

    DRAMATIC WORKS, now printed for the first time with a specially designed title-page and binding to each volume, by CHARLES SHANNON. 500 copies 7s. 6d net. Also 50 copies large paper, 15s. net.

    Vol. I. LADY WINDERMERE'S FAN. A comedy in four acts.
    Vol. II. THE DUCHESS OF PADUA. A blank verse tragedy in five acts.
    Vol. III. A WOMAN OF NO IMPORTANCE. A comedy in four acts. [*In preparation.*

WILDE (OSCAR).

    SALOME: A TRAGEDY IN ONE ACT, done into English, with 10 illustrations, and cover design by AUBREY BEARDSLEY. 500 copies, 15s net. Also 50 copies, large paper, 30s. net.
    [*In preparation.*

WYNNE (FRANCES).

    WHISPER. A volume of Verse. Fcap. 8vo, buckram, 2s. 6d. net
    Transferred by the Author to the Present Publishers.

The Hobby Horse

A new series of this illustrated magazine will be published quarterly by subscription, under the Editorship of Herbert P. Horne. Subscription £1 per annum, post free, for the four numbers. Quarto, printed on hand-made paper, and issued in a limited edition, to subscribers only. The magazine will contain articles upon Literature, Music, Painting, Sculpture, Architecture, and the Decorative Arts; Poems; Essays; Fiction; original Designs; with reproductions of pictures and drawings by the old masters and contemporary artists. There will be a new title-page and ornaments designed by the Editor. Among the contributors to the Hobby Horse are:

THE LATE MATTHEW ARNOLD.	F. YORK POWELL.
LAWRENCE BINYON.	CHRISTINA G. ROSSETTI.
WILFRID BLUNT.	W. M. ROSSETTI.
FORD MADOX BROWN.	JOHN RUSKIN, D.C.L., LL.D.
THE LATE ARTHUR BURGESS.	FREDERICK SANDYS.
E. BURNE-JONES, A.R.A.	THE LATE W. BELL SCOTT.
AUSTIN DOBSON.	FREDERICK J. SHIELDS.
RICHARD GARNETT, LL.D.	J H. SHORTHOUSE.
A. J. HIPKINS, F.S.A.	JAMES SMETHAM.
SELWYN IMAGE.	SIMEON SOLOMON.
LIONEL JOHNSON.	A. SOMERVELL.
RICHARD LE GALLIENNE.	THE LATE J. ADDINGTON SYMONDS.
SIR F. LEIGHTON, Bart., P.R.A.	KATHARINE TYNAN.
T. HOPE MCLACHLAN.	G. F. WATTS, R.A.
MAY MORRIS.	FREDERICK WEDMORE.
C. HUBERT H. PARRY, Mus. Doc.	OSCAR WILDE.
A. W. POLLARD.	ETC. ETC.

Prospectus on application.

THE BODLEY HEAD, VIGO STREET, LONDON, W.

"Nearly every book put out by MESSRS. ELKIN MATHEWS AND JOHN LANE, at the sign of the Bodley Head, is a satisfaction to the special senses of the modern bookman for bindings, shapes, types, and papers. They have surpassed themselves and registered a real achievement in English book-making by the volume of 'Poems, Dramatic and Lyrical' of Lord De Tabley."—*Newcastle Daily Chronicle.*

www.ingramcontent.com/pod-product-compliance
Lightning Source LLC
Chambersburg PA
CBHW020253170426
43202CB00008B/344